100 GREATS GLAMORGAN COUNTY CRICKET CLUB

Some of the stars from Glamorgan's great team of the late 1940s.

100 GREATS

GREATS

GLAMORGAN
COUNTY CRICKET CLUB

WRITTEN BY
ANDREW HIGNELL

TEMPUS

First published 2000
Copyright © Andrew Hignell, 2000

Tempus Publishing Limited
The Mill, Brimscombe Port,
Stroud, Gloucestershire, GL5 2QG

ISBN 0 7524 1879 3

Typesetting and origination by
Tempus Publishing Limited
Printed in Great Britain by
Midway Clark Printing, Wiltshire

Statistical Note:

All the career statistics are correct to 1 April 2000, and refer to performances for Glamorgan CCC in first-class cricket since 1921, the Sunday/National League, the Benson and Hedges Cup, the Gillette Cup and the NatWest Trophy, as well as Minor County matches between 1889 and 1920.

Key:

Statistics in normal text denote first-class records in three- or four-day cricket since 1921. Those in italics show a player's one-day record, while those in brackets are for when a player was competing for Glamorgan in Minor County cricket, prior to 1921. The full ground names of Sophia Gardens, Cardiff, and Cardiff Arms Park have been abbreviated to Sophia Gardens and Arms Park. Data for five wickets in an innings and ten wickets in a match does not include one-day fixtures. The letters at the top of the page refer to the following batting or bowling styles:

RHB – right-handed batsman
LHB – left-handed batsman
OB – off-spinner
SLA – slow left arm spin
RFM – right-arm fast medium
RF – right-arm fast
LF – left-arm fast
LM – left-arm medium pace
RM – right-arm medium pace
LB – leg spinner
WK – wicketkeeper

PREFACE

This book outlines the deeds of 100 out of the 523 people, both professionals and amateurs, who have represented Glamorgan in first-class and minor-county cricket from 1889 to 1999. A few wags might ask whether a county that has won the County Championship on just three occasions, won the Sunday League title once and played in two Lord's finals, could produce such a number of great cricketers. Such doubts certainly don't exist and, as this book shows, Glamorgan CCC has possessed some truly great players.

It should not be forgotten that this is my own personal choice and there might be some people who would argue over the inclusion of a few names. In order to produce my selection, I have used great actions or deeds by the county's players as the yardstick in addition to record-breaking feats and unique achievements either on or off the field for Glamorgan or the world of cricket in general. I have also ignored those players whose contributions were great for other counties or England rather than for Glamorgan. Therefore, to retain a Welsh focus, I have not included the likes of Chris Smith, Mike Selvey, Robin Hobbs and Chris Cowdrey, all of whom achieved fame before, or after, their short playing careers with the Welsh club.

Few will argue against the inclusion of players such as Hugh Morris, Matthew Maynard, Steve Watkin, Maurice Turnbull and Johnnie Clay, all of whom would have been great players, no matter which county they played for, or the likes of Alan Jones, Wilf Wooller and Don Shepherd, even though they never won any Test caps for England.

Others, such as Tom Whittington and George Lavis, more than merit inclusion, despite their modest first-class record. Both warrant a place in any book paying tribute to Glamorgan players, given the context of their immense contribution to the county club off the field. If it had not been for Whittington's lobbying efforts with the MCC authorities after the Great War, Glamorgan might never have risen to the ranks of the first-class world. Lavis played his role much later, as a coach helping to groom a steady stream of junior players, overseeing their transition from colts into fully-fledged county players.

I have also looked ahead to the future and included several players who, at the time of publication, have yet to scale the heights. The likes of Dean Cosker and Mike Powell are young cricketers who I feel are destined to become great Glamorgan players in the next few years and therefore deserve inclusion in this book.

ACKNOWLEDGEMENTS

My thanks first of all to Robert Croft for writing the foreword and to James Howarth of Tempus Publishing for the initial ideas, and his subsequent support in producing this book. The photographs are drawn chiefly from the club's official archives, but I am grateful to several people for providing excellent images, including: Huw John, Bob Harragan, Steve Kloppe, the late David Lemmon, George Herringshaw and David Scranage of Associated Sports Photography, David Smith, Owain Howell, John Morgan, Peter Davies, John Jenkins and Mrs E.H. Parker-Jervis. My thanks also to Mike Fatkin and Tony Dilloway of Glamorgan CCC for their help in providing unlimited access to the club archives, to Edward Bevan and to my wife Debra for her help in the preparation of the manuscript for this book. Lastly, but by no means least, my thanks to the many players of Glamorgan CCC whose wonderful deeds actually made possible a book of this nature.

Andrew Hignell
June 2000

WHO WERE THE GREATEST?

In the winter and spring of 2000, Glamorgan members took part in a vote to nominate who, in their opinion, was the greatest player in each of nine categories. The result of the vote was:

Opening Batsman	Alan Jones
Middle-Order Batsman	Matthew Maynard
Fast Bowler	Steve Watkin
Slow/Spin Bowler	Don Shepherd
All-Rounder	Allan Watkins
Captain	Wilf Wooller
Wicketkeeper	Eifion Jones
Fielder	Peter Walker
Overseas Player	Viv Richards

Add to these nine the likes of Hugh Morris, Johnnie Clay, Tony Lewis or Gilbert Parkhouse and what a wonderful eleven they would make.

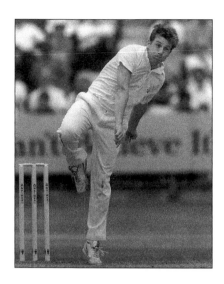

FOREWORD

There are many descriptions of the word 'great' in the Oxford Dictionary such as genius, remarkable ability, beyond the ordinary and so on. Indeed, one has to be careful to exaggerate when certain deeds are performed. But, looking through this book of Glamorgan players and thinking of the international cricketers that I have played against, I doubt whether anyone would disagree with my particular choice of the 'great ones'.

Let us start with our own two Welsh greats, both of whom played in the same era, but unbelievably were not selected for England. Alan Jones did play once but, despite competing against a Rest of the World team which included some of the greatest players in history (including Sobers, Procter and Barry Richards among others), the authorities decided afterwards that the event did not warrant Test status and Alan's name was removed from the records. I was fortunate to see him bat against the world's best and his tally of over 35,000 runs is testimony of his great skill and courage over 27 loyal seasons with Glamorgan. After he finished his career I was ever grateful for the technical advice he passed on to me when he led the Glamorgan Colts team and when he was club coach.

Another legend in Glamorgan history is Don Shepherd. His record of over 2,200 wickets at an average of less than 21 is likely to stand – if not forever – for many years, given the present structure of the first-class game. He was a wonderful bowler and, like Alan, has helped me considerably and continues to do so whether on the practise field, in the commentary box or at the bar at close of play.

Alan and Don were two great Glamorgan cricketers, but what of the others worldwide? The five greatest batsmen I have bowled against are Sachin Tendulkar, the Waugh twins (Steve and Mark), Brian Lara and Graham Gooch. I will never forget Lara's first innings for Warwickshire when he scored 147 against Glamorgan at Edgbaston. It was a masterly innings and bowling at him that day I got the impression he was purposely playing the ball a yard either side of the fielder. Gooch could destroy an attack, while the Waughs are different in style and method but equally as destructive. I have left the best until last – the little master Tendulkar. He was described to me once by Ravi Shastri when he made his debut as a sixteen-year-old boy as 'someone sent from above'. I now know what Ravi meant and have no hesitation in naming the little maestro from Bombay as 'the greatest'.

Robert Croft

100 GLAMORGAN GREATS

Tony Allin
Trevor Arnott
Billy Bancroft
Steve Barwick
William Bates
John Bell
Joseph Brain
William Brain
Tom Brierley
Alan Butcher
Tom Cartwright
Johnnie Clay
Phil Clift
George Cording
Tony Cordle
Dean Cosker
Tony Cottey
Harry Creber
Robert Croft
Adrian Dale
Edmund David
Dai Davies
Emrys Davies
Haydn Davies
Roger Davis
Winston Davis
Dick Duckfield
Arnold Dyson
David Evans
Trevor Every
Roy Fredericks
Roy Gabe-Jones
Ted Glover
Hugh Griffiths

Bernard Hedges
David Hemp
Norman Hever
Vernon Hill
Geoff Holmes
John Hopkins
Steve James
Javed Miandad
Viv Jenkins
Alan Jones
Alan Lewis Jones
Closs Jones
Eifion Jones
Jeff Jones
Willie Jones
Peter Judge
Jacques Kallis
George Lavis
Roland Lefebvre
Tony Lewis
Euros Lewis
Mike Llewellyn
Willie Llewelyn
Jim McConnon
Majid Khan
Austin Matthews
Matthew Maynard
Jack Mercer
Colin Metson
Herbie Morgan
J. Trevil Morgan
Hugh Morris
Ezra Moseley
Len Muncer

Jack Nash
Malcolm Nash
Rodney Ontong
Gilbert Parkhouse
Frank Pinch
Mike Powell
Jim Pressdee
Alan Rees
Gwyn Richards
Viv Richards
Norman Riches
Frank Ryan
Ravi Shastri
Don Shepherd
Cyril Smart
Billy Spiller
Jimmy Stone
Jock Tait
Greg Thomas
Darren Thomas
Stan Trick
Maurice Turnbull
Peter Walker
Cyril Walters
Waqar Younis
Steve Watkin
Allan Watkins
Ossie Wheatley
Tom Whittington
Alan Wilkins
Lawrence Williams
Wilf Wooller

The top 20, who appear here in italics, are each covered on two pages instead of the usual one.

Tony Allin

RHB and SLA, 1976

Born: Barnstaple, 20 April 1954

Batting career:

M	I	NO	Runs	Av
13	16	8	108	13.50
3	*2*	*1*	*8*	*8.00*

50	100	CT/ST
–	–	3
–	–	–

Bowling career:

O	M	R	W	Av
333.3	96	1011	44	22.97
17.4	*1*	*88*	*3*	*29.33*

5wI	10wM
4	1

Career best performances:
32 v Somerset, Weston-Super-Mare, 1976
8/63 v Sussex, Sophia Gardens, 1976
8* v Kent, Canterbury, 1976
1/22 v Kent, Canterbury, 1976

Tony Allin nearly made a fairytale rise from the ranks of Minor County cricket to the heady world of Test cricket during his debut season with Glamorgan in 1976. Sadly, it proved not to be and 1976 was his one and only summer with the county. Had it not been for the turmoil within the club at that time, the left-arm spin bowler would have certainly played in more than 13 matches, and probably gone on to stake a very strong claim for inclusion in the England side.

Allin was brought up in North Devon and initially played with great promise for both Belmont College, Barnstaple, and the local club. He showed immense potential as a spin bowler and made his debut for Devon in 1972. His subsequent success in Minor County cricket attracted the attention of Glamorgan's talent scouts and he joined the county in 1976.

The spinner made his first-class debut against Essex in mid-May at Swansea. Rain ruined the game and he did not get a chance to bowl until the following match against Leicestershire, also at St Helen's. Allin duly claimed the wicket of John Steele in an impressive spell of controlled

spin and continued to make great headway with seven wickets against Gloucestershire at Cheltenham, before taking 8/63 in the match against Sussex at Cardiff, dismissing England captain Tony Greig in both innings.

He continued to prosper during August, with returns of 6/133 and 5/95 from 66 overs of intelligent spin bowling in the match against Middlesex at Swansea. He followed this with the fine figures of 21.2-11-24-6 in the match at Worcestershire and his name began to be touted as a contender for a place on England's winter tour to India. However, Allin was not included in the tour party and by the end of the summer he had also left the Welsh county, disenchanted with life as a professional cricketer.

It had been an uneasy summer for Glamorgan, there were rumours of discontent in the dressing room and, midway through the long, hot summer of 1976, captain Majid Khan quit the club. It was not surprising that Allin opted for a more peaceful life on his father's dairy farm and playing Minor County cricket for Devon, away from all the bickering and backbiting.

Trevor Arnott

RHB and RM, 1921-1930

Born: Radyr, 16 February 1902
Died: Ross-on-Wye, 2 February 1975

Batting career:

M	I	NO	Runs	Av
188	321	25	4726	15.96

50	100	CT/ST
15	3	87

Bowling career:

O	M	R	W	Av
3697.3	642	11435	361	31.68

5wI	10wM
10	–

Career best performances:
153 v Essex, Swansea, 1928
7/40 v West Indians, Arms Park, 1923

Trevor Arnott was a regular in the Glamorgan side between 1921 and 1930 and, despite several heavy defeats, he led the county in 1928 with a calm and debonair authority. He had also made a name for himself in 1926 during the match with Somerset at the Arms Park by becoming the first Glamorgan cricketer to claim a hat-trick in the County Championship.

Educated at Monmouth School and Wycliffe College, Arnott was a typical sporting gentleman of the inter-war era. Besides bowling at a lively medium pace and hitting the ball hard in Glamorgan's middle order, Arnott played club rugby for Cardiff, owned several successful greyhounds and was a more-than-useful golfer.

His bold and carefree hitting reflected his happy-go-lucky outlook and he recorded some rapid centuries – his maiden century against Derbyshire at Swansea in 1924 came in only 75 minutes, with Arnott reaching this personal landmark in the grand manner, with a mighty six onto the roof of the St Helen's grandstand.

He followed this with 126 against Surrey at The Oval in 1927 and a career best 153 against

Essex in 1928. In 1927 he accumulated 728 runs, his highest seasonal aggregate, and he could have scored over 1,000 had he been give more support. It was a similar story with the ball: Glamorgan's poor form meant Arnott rarely bowled in both innings of a match. Overall, his most successful season for bowling was in 1923 when he claimed 64 victims, including spells of 5/50 against Surrey, 6/98 against Yorkshire and a career best 7/40 in the victory over the West Indians as the tourists perished playing some loose strokes against Arnott's brisk seamers.

Arnott was a close friend of Johnnie Clay and had no hesitation in agreeing to stand in as the county's captain in 1928 when Clay's business commitments prevented him from leading the side regularly. He also played for the Gentlemen and Incogniti, and his popularity on the county circuit and jolly attitude led to many invitations to join private tours. Among his overseas trips were visits to Jamaica with Tennyson's XI in 1927/28 and to South America with Sir Julian Cahn's XI in 1929/30. After retiring from county cricket, Arnott coached at Monmouth School.

Billy Bancroft

RHB and RM, 1889-1914

Born: Swansea, 2 March 1871
Died: Swansea, 3 March 1959

Batting career:

M	I	NO	Runs	Av
(230	357	19	8250	24.41)

50	100	CT/ST
(39	7	185/2)

Bowling career:

O	M	R	W	Av
(47.0	12	170	10	17.00)

5wI	10wM
(1	–)

Career best performances:
(207 v Berkshire, Swansea, 1903)
(5/20 v Surrey 2nd XI, Swansea, 1899)

Billy Bancroft was Glamorgan's first professional player and one of Wales's leading sportsmen during the late Victorian and Edwardian era. A cobbler by trade, Bancroft played rugby and cricket for his native Swansea, often alongside his father William, who was a leading player with the early Glamorganshire club. Bancroft won 33 rugby caps in consecutive internationals from 1890 until 1901, playing chiefly at full-back. His amazing kicking, in the era of heavy leather balls, was legendary, with Bancroft being able to drop or place-kick a ball with unerring accuracy.

He made his debut as an eighteen year old in Glamorgan's first ever match in 1889 against Warwickshire at Cardiff Arms Park and regularly won selection in the Glamorgan side for their subsequent friendlies. In 1894 he hit four half-centuries and then in 1896 he recorded his maiden century, against Monmouthshire at Newport. By this time, the Welsh county were looking to appoint their first ever professional cricketer and it was fitting that the committee opted for the multi-talented Bancroft.

Bancroft didn't let the Glamorgan officials

down as he developed into one of the finest all-rounders in Minor County cricket, batting and bowling right-handed, and also keeping wicket if Glamorgan were short of a specialist 'keeper. He produced a fine all-round performance against the Surrey 2nd XI in 1899 at Swansea, hitting 102 and then taking 5/20 with his off-cutters. In 1903 Bancroft recorded a superb double century on his home ground against Berkshire and repeatedly went down the wicket to hit some spectacular drives. The Berkshire bowlers were on the receiving end again in 1905 as Bancroft made 105 against them at Reading.

During his Glamorgan career Bancroft scored 8,250 runs, which also included 157 against Devon at Swansea in 1908 and 109 against Cornwall at the same ground in 1909. It was fitting that some of his finest performances were on his home ground where he carefully prepared the St Helen's wicket for many years. After retiring from county cricket in 1914, Bancroft helped to coach many young players, including Gilbert Parkhouse, who went on to play Test cricket for England.

Steve Barwick
RHB and RM, 1981-1996

Born: Neath, 6 September 1960				

Batting career:

M	I	NO	Runs	Av
212	203	74	873	6.77
264	*97*	*55*	*349*	*8.31*

50	100	CT/ST		
–	–	47		
–	*–*	*38*		

Bowling career:

O	M	R	W	Av
6096.0	1701	16186	456	35.50
1989.1	*172*	*8245*	*304*	*27.12*

5wI	10wM
10	1

Career best performances:
30 v Hampshire, Bournemouth, 1988
8/42 v Worcestershire, Worcester, 1983
48 v Worcestershire, Worcester, 1989*
6/28 v Derbyshire, Derby, 1993

The accurate bowling of Steve Barwick was a vital ingredient in Glamorgan's one-day attack in the late 1980s and early 1990s, and his miserly attitude to conceding runs was a key feature in Glamorgan securing the AXA League title in 1993. In the opening game of the season he took a career best 6/28 against Derbyshire and, throughout the summer, Barwick's subtle off-cutters and change of pace teased and tormented many of the finest batsmen on the county circuit. Some writers even suggested that the England selectors could do far worse than picking Barwick in their side for one-day internationals.

Steve Barwick joined the county in 1981 as a fast-medium seam bowler. Two years later he took a career best 8/42 against Worcestershire at the New Road ground. The following season he passed 50 wickets for the first time and prospered again at Worcester, with 7/55 in the victory over Worcestershire. 'Basil' was awarded his county cap in 1987 and in 1989 he experimented with off-cutters in the style of the legendary Don Shepherd. In the match against Somerset at Taunton, he took advice on field placing from

'Shep' during the lunch break, before going out to take 7/47 and record a ten-wicket match haul for the first and only time in his career.

The 1989 season proved to be Barwick's most successful in first-class cricket as he finished the year with 64 wickets. He wisely decided to concentrate on off-cutters during the 1990s, especially as there were few other bowlers of this style in either the Championship or one-day games. So highly was Barwick regarded by opponents that some teams even held meetings to specifically talk about how they were going to play him. A few bowlers with other counties also tried to copy his style, with one even announcing to his captain that he was going to bowl 'Basils'!

Towards the end of his career, Barwick's appearances were restricted to one-day games, as the Glamorgan selectors opted for more wicket-taking bowlers in Championship cricket. Despite his infrequent appearances, Barwick remained one of the country's most economical bowlers in limited-overs competition. He took a well-deserved benefit year in 1995 and was released from the staff at the end of the 1996 season.

Born: Kirkheaton, 5 March 1884				
Died: Belfast, 17 January 1957				

Batting career:

M	I	NO	Runs	Av
283	500	15	12600	25.97
(6	10	0	202	20.20)

50	100	CT/ST
66	10	182
(–	–	–)

Bowling career:

O	M	R	W	Av
2101.4	202	8408	224	37.53
(82.1	14	299	15	19.93)

5wI	10wM
4	–

Career best performances:
200* v Worcestershire, Kidderminster,1927
8/93 v Essex, Leyton, 1928
(44 v Cheshire, Aigburgh, 1920)
(6/119 v Surrey 2nd XI, The Oval, 1920)

William Bates was the first of many successful signings from other counties as the Glamorgan officials sought to strengthen their playing resources in their bid for first-class status. Bates joined Glamorgan in 1914 after a brief spell with his native Yorkshire; the prospect of regular Championship cricket was the main attraction behind his move to South Wales.

The right-handed batsman had played 113 times for Yorkshire between 1907 and 1913, before joining Briton Ferry Steel CC and qualifying for the Welsh side. By the time Glamorgan were admitted to the County Championship in 1921, Bates had won a regular place in their team and was developing into a most reliable opening batsman.

In 1923 he achieved the feat of scoring 1,000 runs for the season without scoring a century, whilst in 1927 he became the first Glamorgan batsman to record a century in each innings, with 105 and 111 against Essex at Leyton. The following year, it was Bates the left-arm spinner who teased the Essex side, taking a career best 8/93 at the same ground.

Bates's most productive season was in 1927, when he scored 200* against Worcestershire at Kidderminster as well as centuries against Nottinghamshire and the two at Leyton, to finish the summer with 1,645 runs. He also passed the 1,500 run mark in 1928, and began a prolific partnership with fellow Tyke, Arnold Dyson. Indeed, the pair must have taken great delight in sharing a stand of 233 for the first wicket against Yorkshire at Sheffield in 1930. Bates also developed into a most reliable fielder close to the wicket and in 1928 he set a club record by claiming five catches in the innings against Warwickshire at Edgbaston.

Financial problems in the early 1930s meant that the county had to cut their playing staff and Bates was one of several seasoned professionals whose services had to be dispensed with to save money in 1931. He continued his playing career with Cheshire in the Minor County Championship before becoming a groundsman and coach in Northern Ireland. Bates was also a useful footballer in his youth, playing for Bolton and Leeds United.

John Bell
RHB,1924-1931

Born: Batley, 16 June 1895
Died: Guiseley, 14 August 1974

Batting career:

M	I	NO	Runs	Av
166	281	18	7324	27.84

50	100	CT/ST
34	10	61

Bowling career:

O	M	R	W	Av
43.2	3	205	2	102.50

5wI	10wM
–	–

Career best performances:
225 v Worcestershire, Dudley, 1926
1/2 v Sussex, Hove, 1930

John Bell was another Yorkshireman who joined Glamorgan in the 1920s after failing to secure a regular place in his native county's team. The Batley-born batsman played just seven times for Yorkshire between 1921 and 1923, before deciding to move to South Wales, where he enjoyed a successful career for his adopted county.

The qualification rules prevented Bell from playing in Championship cricket in 1924, but he showed great promise on his debut against the touring South Africans and during 1925 he developed into a correct and workmanlike batsman. He moved up to open the batting in 1926 and responded with a career best 225 against Worcestershire at Dudley, besides sharing a rapid partnership of 177 in just 70 minutes with wicketkeeper Trevor Every.

He passed 1,500 runs in his first full season as an opener and more than justified his promotion with other centuries against Warwickshire, Northamptonshire and Somerset. He had a modest year in 1927, but returned to form in 1928 with a career best aggregate of 1,551 runs, with centuries against Leicestershire and Nottinghamshire, as well as eight other half-centuries. Bell also played for Wales in their first-class games between 1924 and 1930, and in 1927 he struck 209 against the MCC, confirming his ability to compile long and steady innings.

Bell was particularly strong off his legs and frequently drove powerfully in an arc from mid-wicket to mid-on. He was, however, less effective on the off-side and this weakness started to be exposed during 1930 and 1931 as the county bowlers learned not to bowl down the leg-side to Bell. He consequently failed to pass 1,000 runs in these two summers and when Glamorgan's committee faced the difficult decision in 1931 of saving money by pruning their professional staff, Bell was one of the players to leave the club.

After the Second World War, Bell briefly returned to county cricket, standing as an umpire before retiring in 1951 and becoming a male nurse at Menston Hospital.

Born: Bristol, 11 September 1863
Died: Bonvilston, 26 June 1914

Batting career:

M	I	NO	Runs	Av
(145	225	17	5236	25.17)

50	100	CT/ST
(19	5	111/50)

Bowling career:

O	M	R	W	Av
(99.4	20	317	20	15.85)

5wI	10wM
(1	–)

Career best performances:
(144 v MCC, Lord's, 1896)
(6/62 v Hill's XI, Arms Park, 1895)

Joseph Brain was the man responsible for Glamorgan becoming a fully-fledged Minor County in 1897. Through his efforts on and off the field, he helped to mould a very successful side, who shared the Minor County title in 1900, and on three later occasions reached the knockout final of the Minor County competition.

Brain attended Clifton College, where he soon displayed immense promise as a gifted right-handed batsman. In 1883 the youngster made his county debut for Gloucestershire, before going to Oxford, where he won four Blues. Brain was also in the Varsity eleven which defeated the 1884 Australians and, later that summer, he hit 108 for Gloucestershire against the tourists to confirm his standing as one of the finest young batsmen in the West Country.

After leaving Oxford, Brain joined his family's brewing business and in 1890 he was promoted to oversee their successful operations in Cardiff. The following season he made his Glamorgan debut and took over the captaincy.

Over the next two decades, he became their leading batsman, with 1901 and 1902 being his most productive seasons, topping 500 runs on both occasions. During 1902 Brain played a series of elegant innings, including 107 against Berkshire at the Arms Park and 69 in the return fixture at Reading, as well as a forceful 67 against Warwickshire at Edgbaston. Indeed, Brain was the only Glamorgan batsman to look comfortable in this friendly against first-class opponents. In all games for the Welsh county, Brain scored over 5,000 runs, which included a career best 144 against the MCC at Lord's in 1896. He also kept wicket when other 'keepers were unavailable.

Brain's efforts were not restricted to the field, as he became an influential figure when the side sought first-class status. He acted as secretary from 1891 to 1908 and was instrumental in Glamorgan's elevation into the Minor County Championship in 1897. He also used his business contacts to secure money for the club and decent job opportunities for some of the professionals. Sadly, Brain died after a short illness in June 1914 before the fruits of his labours saw Glamorgan's elevation to the first-class ranks.

William Brain

RHB and WK, 1896-1908

Born: Clifton, Bristol, 21 July 1870
Died: Dinas Powis, 20 December 1934

Batting career:

M	I	NO	Runs	Av
(105	155	17	2257	16.36)

50	100	CT/ST
(6	2	122/118)

Career best performance:
(113 v Monmouthshire, Newport, 1897)

William Brain was Glamorgan's first regular 'keeper in the Minor County Championship. In 1893 he had created a unique record, when playing for Gloucestershire, by making three stumpings in consecutive deliveries as Charles Townsend took a hat-trick against Somerset at Cheltenham College.

Like his older brother Joseph, he was educated at Clifton College, before going to Oxford and joining the family's brewing business in South Wales during the mid-1890s. Brain's agile wicketkeeping, coupled with his bold and uninhibited strokeplay in the middle order, secured him a regular place in the Glamorgan side from 1896.

During his career, Brain hit two centuries, against Monmouthshire at Newport in 1897 and against Berkshire at the Arms Park in 1901. By the time he retired in 1908, Brain had 175 dismissals to his name in Minor County Championship cricket, with 90 stumpings. This record spoke volumes for his deft glovework and was a testament to the quality of Glamorgan's spin attack. Indeed, in four seasons, he took more

stumpings than catches, as opposing batsmen struggled against the wiles of Harry Creber's left-arm spin and the off-spinners of Jack Nash.

William Brain's tally of 20 stumpings in 1901 and 1903 still figures amongst the highest taken in a season by a Glamorgan wicketkeeper. Indeed, several writers of the time believe that Brain could have gone on to win Test honours if he had been able to play regularly in the County Championship.

Brain served on the Glamorgan committee from 1901 until his business commitments forced his retirement from the Minor County side in 1908. He was subsequently appointed chairman of Brains Brewery in 1914, but continued to play club cricket for Cardiff and the MCC.

He also took great delight in the way two of his sons – Michael and Pat – both kept wicket in first-class cricket for the Welsh county. Michael made one appearance against Oxford University in 1930, whilst Pat appeared in six matches between 1921 and 1928 and, like his father and uncle, was always ready to help out the county whenever they were short of players.

Tom Brierley
RHB and WK, 1931-1939

Born: Southampton, 15 June 1910
Died: Vancouver, 7 January 1989

Batting career:

M	I	NO	Runs	Av
181	292	25	4760	17.82

50	100	CT/ST
20	3	153/72

Bowling career:

O	M	R	W	Av
5.0	0	33	0	–

5wI	10wM
–	–

Career best performance:
116 v Lancashire, Old Trafford, 1938

Tom Brierley was Glamorgan's first ever player to have a successful coaching career overseas, and the former Glamorgan batsman opened the batting for his adopted Canada against the Pakistani tourists at Lord's in 1954.

Brierley was also one of the few Glamorgan players of the inter-war era to secure a contract with another English county. Having played for Glamorgan from 1931 until 1939, he joined Lancashire after the Second World War, and made 46 appearances between 1946 and 1948. Another curiosity in Brierley's career was that he made his career best score of 116 for Glamorgan against Lancashire at Old Trafford in 1938, and then equalled it for his new county against Glamorgan at Liverpool in 1947.

Brierley had initially joined the Glamorgan staff in the early 1930s as a specialist batsman, but he won a regular place as a wicketkeeper from 1934, following Trevor Every's retirement because of deteriorating sight. Brierley proved to be a competent 'keeper, claiming 21 catches and 19 stumpings in his first season behind the stumps.

Brierley recorded a maiden Championship hundred against Sussex in 1937 and also made 62 dismissals, including 24 stumpings, chiefly from the clever spin of Johnnie Clay. Despite his success as a 'keeper, Brierley decided to hand over the gauntlets to Haydn Davies in 1938, generously realising that he represented the club's future. Brierley's batting still secured him a regular place in Maurice Turnbull's side and in 1938 he topped the 1,000 mark, thanks to 6 half-centuries and his century against Lancashire.

In 1946 Brierley accepted an offer from Lancashire, as there was a possibility of a coaching position at Old Trafford. However, this did not materialise and at the end of 1948 he decided to emigrate to Canada. He combined teaching economics at Shawnigan Lake School with coaching cricket and duly became one of Canada's leading coaches. He also won a place in their national side and returned to the UK in 1954 as a member of the touring party. His experience of English conditions proved invaluable and, despite being forty-four, he batted with distinction throughout the tour.

Alan Butcher
LHB and LM or SLA, 1987-1992

Born: Croydon, 7 January 1954

Batting career:

M	I	NO	Runs	Av
111	192	17	7899	45.14
95	*93*	*10*	*2492*	*30.02*

50	100	CT/ST
54	17	54
15	*2*	*19*

Bowling career:

O	M	R	W	Av
150.4	20	625	15	41.67
41.1	*2*	*232*	*5*	*46.40*

5wI	10wM
–	–

Career best performances:
171* v Warwickshire, Sophia Gardens, 1989
3/35 v Middlesex, Sophia Gardens, 1987
127 v Yorkshire, Sophia Gardens, 1991
3/32 v Sussex, Swansea, 1989

Alan Butcher shrewdly led Glamorgan between 1989 and 1992, and formed a most effective opening partnership with fellow left-hander Hugh Morris. Their most productive season was in 1990 when the pair shared 11 century opening stands, with Butcher amassing 2,116 runs, and by scoring 15 fifties he set a new club record for the most number of Championship half-centuries made in any season.

Butcher had joined Glamorgan in 1987 after a highly successful career with Surrey, during which he won a Test cap against India at The Oval in 1979. He had initially joined the Surrey staff in 1972 as a left-arm seam bowler, but in the mid-1970s he became John Edrich's opening partner, and by the 1980s was one of the most consistent openers on the county circuit.

Butcher's most productive season with Surrey was 1980, as he compiled 1,713 runs (including a career best 216* against Cambridge University) whilst in 1984 he scored a century in each innings at The Oval against Glamorgan. In 1985 Butcher took a benefit year with Surrey,

before joining Glamorgan in 1987. He continued to be a prolific run-scorer with the Welsh county, and in both 1989 and 1990 he was the first English batsman to reach 1,000 runs for the season. In 1990 he topped the 2,000 mark for the first time in his career, and his thoroughly professional efforts earned him the accolade of being one of *Wisden's* Five Cricketers of the Year.

In 1992 Butcher sustained a serious calf injury which ultimately led to his retirement from the county game. He went on to take coaching jobs with Essex, and subsequently Surrey, for whom he reappeared in 1998 when the county were badly affected by injuries. On the same day as the forty-four year old's surprise return to first-class cricket, his son Mark was opening the batting for England. In 1991 the two had created a county record when they played against each other in the Sunday League match between Glamorgan and Surrey at The Oval. His other son Gary was also on the Glamorgan staff from 1994 until 1998, before joining Mark at Surrey.

Tom Cartwright MBE
RHB and RM, 1977

Born: Coventry, 22 July 1935

Batting career:

M	I	NO	Runs	Av
7	11	2	76	8.44
19	*8*	*4*	*32*	*8.00*

50	100	CT/ST
–	–	2
–	–	2

Bowling career:

O	M	R	W	Av
131.3	52	258	10	25.80
152.0	*26*	*503*	*17*	*29.59*

5wI	10wM
–	–

Career best performances:
22* v Kent, Swansea, 1977
4/46 Yorkshire, Sophia Gardens, 1977
10 v Derbyshire, Sophia Gardens, 1977*
3/17 v Northants, Northampton, 1977

Tom Cartwright MBE was one of the finest medium-pace bowlers in county cricket in the late 1950s and 1960s. In ten seasons with Warwickshire, he took over 1,000 wickets, despite rarely using, or wanting, the new ball. His repertoire of in-swingers and subtle changes of pace also won him 5 Test caps in 1964/65.

Cartwright made his debut for his native Warwickshire in 1952, and over the course of the next two decades he teased the finest of county batsmen with intelligent seam bowling, delivered from a smooth action and a high, rhythmical leap in his delivery stride. He initially gained success with late in-swingers, before adding sharp out-swingers and a variety of cutters. Few batsmen ever managed to dominate his bowling and he could be a most daunting prospect on a green or crumbling wicket.

In 1969 Cartwright took a hat-trick for Warwickshire against Somerset at Edgbaston, but at the end of the summer he joined Millfield School as their cricket coach and transferred his allegiances to Somerset, for whom he played until 1976. In 1977 he joined Glamorgan and was a member of their Gillette Cup final team against Middlesex. The game saw the forty-two year old deliver a characteristically tight spell, finishing with the figures of 12-3-32-1.

He retired from county cricket at the end of the 1977 season, and became Glamorgan's coach and manager. He held these positions until 1980 when he was appointed as Director of Coaching to the Welsh Cricket Association. Since then, his tireless hours of effort and wise guidance have helped to produce a steady stream of talented Welsh cricketers. The fact that several played Test cricket reflects his great contribution to the game in Wales.

Cartwright's career best figures were 8/39 for Warwickshire against Somerset at Weston-Super-Mare in 1962, and his best match figures were 15/89 against Glamorgan at Swansea in 1967. Cartwright was also an effective batsman, scoring a total of 7 first-class centuries. His highest score was 210 for Warwickshire against Middlesex at Nuneaton in 1962, and that season he also completed the coveted double of 1,000 runs and 100 wickets.

Johnnie Clay

RHB and RFM or LB or OB, 1921-1949

Born: Bonvilston, 18 March 1898
Died: St Hilary, 11 August 1973

Batting career:

M	I	NO	Runs	Av
358	536	88	6868	15.33

50	100	CT/ST
17	2	171

Bowling career:

O	M	R	W	Av
9911.1	2326	25181	1292	19.49

5wI	10wM
105	28

Career best performances:
115* v New Zealanders, Arms Park, 1927
9/54 v Northamptonshire, Llanelli, 1935

Without the efforts of Johnnie Clay, Glamorgan CCC might easily have been wound up because of financial problems during the 1930s. Between 1933 and 1938, Clay served as club treasurer and, together with his close friend Maurice Turnbull, he spent winter after winter raising money for the club through special functions. The Cardiff-based businessman also used contacts in the commercial world to good effect and he steered the club through much adversity and ensured that the county remained afloat.

On the field of play, Clay led the bowling attack by example and in 1937 he took 176 wickets – a record which still stands as the most wickets taken in a season for Glamorgan. His efforts also resulted in a call-up into the England squad for the Third, Fourth and Fifth Tests of the series with South Africa in 1935. However, it was not until the final game of the rubber at The Oval that Clay got a chance to win a Test cap, and he typically bowled with commendable accuracy, returning match figures of 32-7-75-0.

Over the next couple of seasons, Clay politely turned down further opportunities at the highest level, suggesting that the selectors chose younger players. Even so, the forty year old was still included in the England party for the First Test of the Ashes series at Trent Bridge in 1938. Clay was rather taken aback that the selectors had ignored his wishes and he withdrew from the squad, telling the chairman of selectors that he was carrying a leg injury and might not last the match. The selectors at long last took the hint that Clay's heart lay with the fortunes of Glamorgan and no other team, and they never called upon his services again.

Educated at Winchester, Clay hailed from a well-known sporting family in the Chepstow area. In his youth, Clay was a tearaway fast bowler, playing initially in Minor County cricket for Monmouthshire, before making his Glamorgan debut in 1921. However, he was affected by a series of injuries and in 1924 he experimented with both leg-breaks and off-spin. He also took over the Glamorgan captaincy and through his enthusiastic efforts the club moved up from the bottom of the Championship table to thirteenth.

Clay was also an aggressive lower-order batsman and played many cavalier innings. In 1927 he hit an unbeaten century against the New Zealand tourists, whilst in 1929 he recorded his maiden Championship hundred against Worcestershire at Swansea. He raced to three figures in just 95 minutes, but what was even more remarkable was that Clay was the number ten batsman – his partnership of 203 with Joe Hills for the ninth wicket is still the club record.

Even late in his career, Clay produced some whirlwind innings – in 1937 he smashed 25 in an over from Sussex's James Langridge, whilst in 1946 he took 24 off an over from India's Vinoo Mankad. Clay could also play the anchor role if needed, as shown by a watchful innings against Lancashire at Old Trafford in 1946. The veteran arrived at the crease with the scoreboard reading 110-7, as Glamorgan chased a target of 164 to win. He played himself in quietly and, together with George Lavis, pushed for ones and twos to see Glamorgan home to a well-earned victory.

Clay's forte was off-spin bowling and the Glamorgan amateur proved to be one of the finest slow bowlers in county cricket either side of the Second World War. He had immaculate powers of flight and spin, and his unerring accuracy forced batsmen to play every ball. Clay would tempt, tease and ultimately trick the finest of players in Championship cricket. On three occasions, he took over 100 wickets, and in 1937 he produced the best ever match figures for Glamorgan of 17/212, after taking 9/66 and 8/146 against Worcestershire at Swansea. He was still an effective bowler in 1946 when Glamorgan regrouped after the Second World War and, following the death of Turnbull, Clay agreed to lead the county as the Championship restarted, keen that his good friend's efforts before the war were not wasted.

During 1946 and 1947 Clay assembled a new squad of players and he helped to groom Wilf Wooller as the county's future leader. He handed over the captaincy to the former Welsh rugby international in 1947 and slipped into semi-retirement. However, with the prospect of the title near, Wooller invited Clay to make a return to the county side for the decisive game against Surrey at the Arms Park. The veteran off-spinner responded with match figures of 10/65, and

J.C. Clay in off-spinning mode in 1938.

remained in the side at Bournemouth as the Welshmen became County Champions for the first time. Indeed, it was fitting that Clay should take the final wicket, trapping the Hampshire number eleven leg before, and there were tears of delight running down his cheeks as he returned to the Dean Park pavilion to celebrate.

Clay was highly regarded by the MCC and served as a Test selector in 1947 and 1948, before playing his final county match aged fifty-one, appropriately enough on Monmouthshire soil against Yorkshire at Newport. He continued to be involved with Glamorgan, serving as a trustee, and from 1960 he was the club's president.

Clay had many other sporting interests, including horse-racing. As a youngster he rode in point-to-points and acted as secretary of the Glamorgan Hunt. In later life, he was a steward and a director of Chepstow Racecourse, which was laid out close to his family's home during the 1920s. A long distance steeplechase is run annually at Chepstow in Clay's memory.

Phil Clift
RHB and OB, 1937-1955

Born: Usk, 3 September 1918

Batting career:

M	I	NO	Runs	Av
183	306	21	6055	21.24

50	100	CT/ST
28	7	169

Bowling career:

O	M	R	W	Av
216.2	38	675	11	61.36

5wl	10wM
–	–

Career best performances:
125* v Derbyshire, Arms Park, 1949
3/6 v Sussex, Llanelli, 1951

Phil Clift served as player, coach and secretary of Glamorgan CCC from 1936 until 1982. The Usk-born player joined the county's playing staff in the mid-1930s as a free-scoring batsman and in 1948 was rated by Don Bradman as being amongst the best young players in the country.

However, Clift suffered from diabetes and bouts of poor health interrupted his playing career soon after his maiden hundred against Nottinghamshire at Trent Bridge in 1947. Even so, he still managed to hit three centuries in 1949 and had a purple patch in mid-June with centuries in consecutive Championship games against Kent and Essex. Indeed, his innings against Essex at Ebbw Vale was probably his greatest for Glamorgan, as the Welsh county were set a stiff target of 177 to win in just 105 minutes. Clift almost single-handedly led the county to victory by nine wickets, and with half an hour to spare! His unbeaten 101 included 2 sixes and 14 crisp fours, as Clift put considerable power and immaculate timing behind a series of forcing strokes on a wearing wicket that the Essex bowlers had hoped to exploit.

As well as playing the role of dashing strokemaker, Clift could also bat for long periods, as shown later in 1949 when he occupied the crease for almost five hours in making a career best 125* against Derbyshire at Cardiff Arms Park. He watchfully saw off the lively Derbyshire seamers and his efforts steered Glamorgan to a comprehensive victory by six wickets.

Clift retired from playing county cricket in 1955 to become the captain of the Second XI and the county's assistant coach, running the indoor schools in Neath and at the Arms Park during the winter months. It was in this capacity that Clift helped to groom many promising young colts, who subsequently went on to a successful playing career with the Welsh county.

In 1959 Clift took over the duties of assistant secretary and he acted as Wilf Wooller's right-hand man in the club's administration. It was therefore fitting that Clift succeeded Wooller in the post of county secretary in 1978, before retiring in 1982 after a lifetime of loyal service to Glamorgan County Cricket Club.

Born: Tredegar, 1 January 1878
Died: St Mellons, 2 February 1946

Batting career:

M	I	NO	Runs	Av
19	34	4	498	16.60
(18	26	1	283	11.32)

50	100	CT/ST
1	1	16/2
(1	–	13/4)

Career best performances:
101 v Worcestershire, Swansea, 1921
(58 v Berkshire, Arms Park, 1900)

George Cording epitomised the spirit among the amateurs who loyally devoted their spare time to Glamorgan during the 1920s. A schoolmaster by profession, Cording was a highly successful batsman at club level and helped the county out as a middle-order batsman and occasional wicketkeeper during his summer holidays. After retiring from playing, he continued to promote the game among the schoolboys of South Wales, creating a steady stream of young talent for Glamorgan to draw upon.

The right-handed batsman first played for the county against Berkshire in 1900, but in the years leading up to the Great War, Cording's teaching commitments, both inside and outside South Wales, restricted his appearances for the county. He became available on a regular basis after the war and continued to be a heavy scorer for the Cardiff club. He was also ready to step in behind the stumps and, indeed, the forty-three-year-old Cording was Glamorgan's wicketkeeper in their inaugural County Championship match in 1921. Despite his grey hairs, the veteran only conceded a handful of byes, and he also showed good form

with the bat. Cording went on to make 101 later in the season against Worcestershire at Swansea, thereby becoming the club's oldest player to hit a maiden Championship century.

Cording captained Cardiff CC in 1921 and 1922, and often invited boys to bowl at him in the outdoor nets at the Arms Park. Before taking guard he would place a penny on each stump and would hand over the coins if one of the pupils dismissed him. Cording helped to promote the game amongst schools in the area, serving as founding chairman of the Welsh Secondary Schools Cricket Association from 1926.

Cording also gave a helping hand to Glamorgan during the Second World War as the club officials attempted to maintain interest in the county. A number of fixtures were therefore arranged during 1944 and 1945 as a means of keeping up the morale of the public, and also to raise funds for the war effort. Despite being well into his sixties, Cording acted as a tireless match secretary, making sure that the cricket-starved public of South Wales got a number of chances to take their minds off the horrors of war.

Tony Cordle
RHB and RFM, 1963-1980

Born: Barbados, 21 September 1940

Batting career:

M	I	NO	Runs	Av
312	433	76	5239	14.67
208	*156*	*37*	*1619*	*13.61*

50	100	CT/ST
9	–	141
2	*–*	*61*

Bowling career:

O	M	R	W	Av
7013.5	1615	19281	701	27.50
1655.0	*215*	*5753*	*217*	*26.51*

5wI	10wM
19	2

Career best performances:
81 v Cambridge University, Margam, 1972
9/49 v Leicestershire, Colwyn Bay, 1969
87 v Nottinghamshire, Trent Bridge, 1971
5/24 v Hampshire, Portsmouth, 1979

Tony Cordle was Glamorgan's first overseas fast bowler and the West Indian was the spearhead of the county's attack which secured the Championship title in 1969. Amongst many fine spells that season, Cordle recorded a career best 9/49 against Leicestershire at Colwyn Bay, when he remarkably came on as seventh change!

Cordle had emigrated from Barbados to the United Kingdom in the early 1960s, having only played club cricket in the Caribbean. He worked briefly with London Transport, before moving to join his brother and sister in Cardiff. A few days later when he went to the Labour Exchange in Westgate Street to secure a job with British Railways, he looked down on the Arms Park cricket ground. Having fond memories of playing cricket back home, Cordle decided to join Cardiff CC, little realising that it was a decision that would transform his life.

After some hostile spells for the Cardiff club, Cordle made his debut that summer for the Second XI and joined the county staff the following season. In 1963 he made his first-class debut against Cambridge University and by 1967 he had won a regular place in the county side, deservedly winning his county cap after taking 74 wickets at 21 apiece.

Cordle had received little coaching in Barbados and played initially as a tearaway fast bowler, bounding in off a long and erratic run. Following advice from Glamorgan's coaches, he cut his run-up and became a skilful and more subtle seamer, bowling on the brisk side of medium. During the 1970s he developed into a fine all-rounder in limited-overs cricket, making useful contributions with bat and ball. In 1979 took a hat-trick in the Sunday League match against Hampshire at Portsmouth, whilst in 1974 he shared a record partnership of 87 for the ninth wicket with Malcolm Nash against Lincolnshire in the Gillette Cup match at Swansea.

Cordle was the Glamorgan beneficiary in 1977 as the club ended a long barren spell by reaching the final of the Gillette Cup. He retired in 1980 and subsequently acted as the county's coach until 1983, when he emigrated to Canada, where he has continued to coach both junior and national teams.

Dean Cosker

RHB and SLA, 1996-present

Born: Weymouth, 7 January 1978

Batting career:

M	I	NO	Runs	Av
48	54	13	396	9.66
45	*26*	*11*	*142*	*9.47*

50	100	CT/ST
–	–	29
–	–	*11*

Bowling career:

O	M	R	W	Av
1303.5	330	3755	99	37.93
318.2	*13*	*1523*	*48*	*31.73*

5wI	10wM
1	–

Career best performances:
49 v Sussex, Sophia Gardens, 1999
6/140 v Lancashire, Colwyn Bay, 1998
27* v Somerset, Taunton, 1999
3/18 v Warwickshire, Edgbaston, 1998

Within months of completing his A-levels at Millfield School in 1996, Dean Cosker was making his Championship debut for Glamorgan against Lancashire at Cardiff. His selection indicated how highly the young left-arm spinner was regarded by Glamorgan's shrewd talent scouts and the Dorset-born bowler could develop into one of the county's top spin bowlers. Indeed, he has already represented England at both under-19 level and England 'A' level and, during the 1996/97 series with Pakistan under-19s, the young bowler so impressed manager Phil Neale with his accuracy and turn that he was included in The Rest XI to play England 'A' in the traditional curtain-raiser for the 1997 season. He was subsequently given an extended run in the Glamorgan side and, with Robert Croft on England duty, he was also given a chance as the county's frontline spinner. The fact that he easily fitted into this role spoke volumes for Cosker's maturity and potential.

Perhaps his finest performance to date came in 1997 during the NatWest quarter-final against Yorkshire at Cardiff. Cosker returned figures of 12-3-26-3 and then shared an unbeaten tenth-wicket partnership of 28 with Waqar Younis to see Glamorgan to a semi-final place. He also delivered many important spells in the four-day matches, as Glamorgan became County Champions, and it was Cosker who took the final wicket of the 1997 campaign, removing Somerset's Ben Trott at Taunton as Glamorgan took the title. Cosker spent the winter of 1997/98 with England 'A' on their tour to East Africa and Sri Lanka, and during 1998 returned career best figures of 6/140 against Lancashire at Colwyn Bay. He also took 3/18 in the floodlit AXA League game against Warwickshire at Edgbaston.

He finished the 1998 season with a decent haul of 36 first-class victims and enjoyed another successful tour in 1998/99 with the England 'A' party in South Africa and Zimbabwe. He had a modest season in 1999, but after a winter off, Cosker will surely fare much better in 2000 and in the years to come.

Tony Cottey
RHB and OB, 1986-1998

Born: Swansea, 2 June 1966

Batting career:

M	I	NO	Runs	Av
197	320	49	10346	38.18
182	*167*	*31*	*3505*	*25.78*

50	100	CT/ST
55	21	137
21	*–*	*66*

Bowling career:

O	M	R	W	Av
167.2	20	704	11	64.00
122.0	*3*	*672*	*19*	*35.37*

5wI	10wM
–	–

Career best performances:
203 v Leicestershire, Swansea, 1994
4/49 v Leicestershire, Swansea, 1996
96 v Sussex, Hove, 1998
4/56 v Essex, Chelmsford, 1992

At 5 feet 4 inches, Tony Cottey is one of the shortest players currently playing county cricket, but few have a bigger heart than the right-handed batsman from Swansea. During the 1990s he became one of the club's most consistent middle-order batsman, scoring 1,465 runs in 1995 and 1,543 in 1996. His gritty determination resulted in many solid innings, and amongst his finest was a remarkable 77 off just 42 balls against Northamptonshire in the AXA League game in 1998. Glamorgan had been set a stiff target of 174 in a mere 24 overs, but Cottey used all of his experience and know-how to lead Glamorgan to victory with three balls in hand.

Cottey is one of the best players of spin bowling in the current first-class game and his nimble footwork, deft sweeping and rock-solid defence have been hallmarks of his play. He had a modest season with the bat during 1997 as Glamorgan became County Champions, but even so, he still shared a match-winning partnership with Matthew Maynard against Essex at Cardiff which helped to guide Glamorgan to a crucial victory. He returned to form in 1998 by passing 1,000 runs in first-class cricket, but at the end of the season he rejected a new two-year deal with Glamorgan and joined Sussex on a five-year contract.

He made his Glamorgan debut in 1986 after a brief, but quite successful, career as a professional footballer with Swansea City, during which time he won Welsh Youth soccer caps. After deciding to concentrate on cricket, Cottey soon established a regular place for himself in the Glamorgan side, as a middle-order batsman and occasional off-spin bowler. He won his county cap in 1992 and in 1996 was appointed the county's vice-captain. The following year, Cottey scored 203 against Leicestershire, fittingly on his home ground at St Helen's where he had first played as a schoolboy with the Swansea club. During this career best innings, Cottey also shared a record seventh-wicket partnership of 211 with Otis Gibson.

Harry Creber

RHB and LM or SLA, 1898-1922

Born: Birkenhead, 30 April 1872
Died: Swansea, 27 March 1939
Batting career:

M	I	NO	Runs	Av
33	58	28	155	5.16
(192	240	80	1665	10.41)

50	100	CT/ST
–	–	6
(1	–	49)

Bowling career:

O	M	R	W	Av
903.5	177	2550	95	26.84
(6271.5	1499	16907	1161	14.56)

5wI	10wM
5	1

Career best performances:
13* v Sussex, Swansea, 1922
7/47 v Hampshire, Swansea, 1922
(53 v Monmouthshire, Newport, 1900)
(9/56 v Carmarthenshire, Llanelli, 1908)

Between 1898 and 1920, Harry Creber was a bowling stalwart in Glamorgan's Minor County side and the left-arm spinner managed to make 33 first-class appearances in the early 1920s. Creber had initially played with distinction for Liverpool CC, before becoming professional groundsman at Swansea CC in 1898. He duly remained at St Helen's until his death in 1939.

He marked his debut season with 31 wickets, before claiming 97 victims in 1899. This haul included a purple patch from the end of June until mid-August, during which Creber took 13/93 against Monmouthshire, 10/88 against the MCC, 12/137 versus Wiltshire and, in the games against Berkshire, 14/147 at Reading followed by 14/124 at the Arms Park.

Further impressive hauls of 13/84 against Wiltshire in 1903 and 11/110 against the same opponents in 1904, were further rewards for Creber's accuracy, subtle spin, and clever variations of pace and flight. However, his greatest prize came in 1905 when he became the club's first bowler to take 100 wickets in a season. His wickets cost just 15 runs apiece and among

his many fine spells were returns of 13/82 against Wiltshire at Chippenham and 11/148 against the MCC at Cardiff Arms Park. Quite fittingly, he claimed his 100th wicket of the season on his home ground at Swansea in Glamorgan's final match of the season against Surrey.

Creber repeated the feat in 1906 with 103 wickets in Minor County matches and claimed 10 wickets in a match on 6 occasions. Twice during his illustrious career, Creber came close to becoming the first Glamorgan player to take ten wickets in an innings. In the 1903 match against the Philadelphians at Cardiff, he took 9/91 against the touring side, and in the 1908 match versus Carmarthenshire, he finished with career best figures of 9/56, as he completely baffled the inexperienced Carmarthenshire batsmen.

Creber was past his best by the time Glamorgan entered the County Championship, but he still managed to claim 95 wickets at the age of fifty, including 7/47 against Hampshire at Swansea in 1922. He retired from county cricket at the end of the 1922 season, but remained in Swansea as groundsman at St Helen's.

Robert Croft

RHB and OB, 1989-present

Born: Morriston, 25 May 1970				
Batting career:				
M	I	NO	Runs	Av
186	275	53	5741	25.86
177	*144*	*37*	*2532*	*23.66*
50	100	CT/ST		
26	2	95		
12	*–*	*46*		
Bowling career:				
O	M	R	W	Av
6621.2	1625	18557	497	37.34
1377.4	*82*	*5680*	*185*	*30.70*
5wI	10wM			
21	3			

Career best performances:
143 v Somerset, Taunton, 1995
8/66 v Warwickshire, Swansea, 1992
77 v Essex, Sophia Gardens, 1998
6/20 v Worcestershire, Sophia Gardens, 1994

Robert Croft has played in more international matches for England than any other Glamorgan cricketer, having played in 15 Test matches and 44 one-day internationals. In 1999 he also became the first Glamorgan player to appear for England in the World Cup competition.

The Welsh-speaking off-spinner made his Glamorgan debut in 1989 and won a regular place in the Welsh county's side as Rodney Ontong was forced into retirement due to injury. Croft's potential was soon recognised by the England selectors, who chose the youngster for the England 'A' tour to the West Indies in 1991/92. The following summer he won his county cap after taking 68 wickets, including 8/66 (with match figures of 14/169) against Warwickshire at Swansea.

He went on the England 'A' tour to South Africa in 1993/94 and developed into a true all-rounder, as testified by a career best 143 against Somerset at Taunton in 1995 and a series of aggressive innings in limited-overs games. His crisp and well- timed strokeplay, allied to his

accurate off-spin, drew the attention of the England selectors in 1996 and he was included in the England side for the final Test of the summer against Pakistan at The Oval.

A steady performance led to a place on the 1996/97 tour to Zimbabwe and New Zealand, where the unflappable Croft turned in some fine performances in both the Tests and one-day games. His accurate off-spin helped England to a series win over the Kiwis and he held his place for the 1997 Ashes series.

In many ways, 1997 was a difficult summer for Robert, with just eight wickets in the series, and an over-exaggerated *contretemps* with Essex's Mark Ilott in the hotly-contested NatWest Trophy semi-final at Chelmsford. But to Robert's delight, Glamorgan became County Champions and the Welshman spent the 1997/98 winter on tour with the England side in Sharjah and the West Indies.

He had limited opportunities in the Caribbean, but returned to the England side for the first three Tests of the series with the South Africans. He was unlucky not to pick up several

Left: *Robert Croft off-drives against Middlesex at Colwyn Bay in June 1995.* Right: *Robert Croft bowling against Durham in the 1983 Natwest Trophy match at Cardiff.*

wickets and, despite a courageous and match-saving innings of 37* in the Third Test at Old Trafford, Croft was dropped from the England Test side. He returned for the one-day triangular series with the Springboks and the Sri Lankans, and then featured in the one-day triangular series with Australia and Sri Lanka after being overlooked for a regular place in the England side during the 1998/99 Ashes tour. Indeed, he continued to be viewed by the English selectors as a one-day specialist and won inclusion in England's squad for the 1999 World Cup.

Croft has also made many useful contributions in one-day games for Glamorgan, often relishing the role of pinch-hitter, with four consecutive half-centuries in the Benson and Hedges competition in 1996. As far as Championship cricket is concerned, Croft holds the record for the most number of balls bowled in a match, delivering a marathon spell of 96 overs against Hampshire at Swansea in 1993. He had another long bowl in the 1999 fixture with Durham at Cardiff, returning match figures of 10/238 from 89.4 overs.

With the England selectors currently looking elsewhere, he is likely to have plenty of work for Glamorgan in the near future. If so, he can set his sights on becoming the first Glamorgan bowler since Don Shepherd to pass the 1,000 wicket mark. Indeed, he is already halfway there after taking his 500th wicket for the county during their Championship match with Gloucestershire at Cardiff in May 2000. This was an especially fitting game for him to reach this landmark as the 2000 season is his benefit year. A few weeks later, Croft also had the opportunity to play in a Lord's final as Glamorgan met Gloucestershire in the final of the Benson & Hedges Cup.

Adrian Dale
RHB and RM, 1989-present

Born: Johannesburg, 24 October 1968

Batting career:

M	I	NO	Runs	Av
173	287	22	8735	32.96
197	*178*	*21*	*4635*	*29.52*

50	100	CT/ST
43	17	68
24	*2*	*47*

Bowling career:

O	M	R	W	Av
1896.5	423	6157	166	37.09
1073.1	*46*	*5375*	*173*	*31.07*

5wI	10wM
2	–

Career best performances:
214* v Middlesex, Sophia Gardens, 1993
6/18 v Warwickshire, Sophia Gardens, 1993
110 v Lincolnshire, Swansea, 1994
6/22 v Durham, Colwyn Bay, 1993

Born in South Africa but raised in Chepstow, Adrian Dale made his Glamorgan debut in 1989 whilst still at Swansea University. A correct right-handed batsman and accurate seam bowler, he was a member of the Glamorgan team who reached the final of the Benson & Hedges Cup at Lord's in June 2000.

Indeed, he has been one of Glamorgan's most successful all-rounders in one-day cricket, scoring over 5,000 runs and taking more than 200 wickets. Only five specialist batsmen have scored more runs and four other bowlers taken more wickets in one-day games for the Welsh county.

Dale's big break came on the pre-season tour to Zimbabwe in 1990/91, where he scored a maiden century in Bulawayo. He was elevated to the number three spot, from which he struck two half-centuries against the touring West Indians, and hit his first Championship hundred against Gloucestershire at Abergavenny. In 1992 he passed 1,000 runs for the first time in his career and recorded an unbeaten 150 against Nottinghamshire at Trent Bridge. His fluent strokeplay and accurate bowling also allowed him to play a pivotal role in the county's one-day team and in 1993 he took 6/22 against Durham at Colwyn Bay, which included a hat-trick.

The 1993 season saw Dale become a member of Glamorgan's side that won the Sunday League title and also share in the highest partnership for any wicket in the club's history. In the Championship match with Middlesex at Sophia Gardens, Dale and Viv Richards shared an unbroken stand of 425 for the fourth wicket. Dale's contribution was a career best 214* and at the end of the season his first-class aggregate was an impressive 1,472 runs. Dale also made centuries against Yorkshire and Worcestershire, and the promising all-rounder was selected for the England 'A' tour to South Africa in 1993/94.

In recent seasons, Dale's bowling has been hampered by niggling back injuries, but he has still made useful contributions with the bat. He recorded a match-winning hundred against Northamptonshire in 1996, passed 1,000 runs again in 1998 and hit 3 centuries in 1999, including 2 in the match with Gloucestershire.

Edmund David

RHB and RM or OB, 1889-1898

Born: St Fagan's, 24 April 1860
Died: Nottage, Porthcawl, 26 July 1942
Batting career:

M	I	NO	Runs	Av
(32	49	3	581	12.63)

50	100	CT/ST
(2	–	19

Bowling career:

O	M	R	W	Av
(87.0	20	268	10	26.80)

5wI	10wM
(–	–)

Career best performances:
(85 v Monmouthshire, Newport, 1896)
(4/48 v Monmouthshire, Newport, 1896)

Edmund David holds a unique place in Glamorgan's history, having led them in their first match against Warwickshire at Cardiff Arms Park in June 1889. He was one of the leading figures in South Wales club cricket in the 1880s and was present at the Angel Hotel on 6 July 1888 when J.T.D. Llewelyn convened a meeting to discuss the formation of Glamorgan CCC.

David agreed to serve on the county's inaugural committee and he drew on his extensive experience of club and country house cricket to help the club assemble a squad of players from which they could field their first ever team. Given his sizeable involvement and social standing, David was a worthy choice as Glamorgan's captain for their first fixture. He also struck the opening blow in the game by winning the toss and electing to bat. However, he and his colleagues struggled against the talented Warwickshire attack and David's contribution was just 0 and 2, as the Welsh county were comfortably defeated.

Despite this modest start, the right-handed batsman secured a regular place in Glamorgan's middle-order for a series of friendlies in their quest for recognition as a Minor County. David had a fine game against Monmouthshire at Newport in 1896 when he produced career best performances with both bat and ball, making 85 and returning 4/48 with his nagging off-cutters. Although past his best, David also figured in Glamorgan's side in 1897, when they were admitted to the Minor County Championship. He played his final Glamorgan game in 1898.

He was the son of William David, the influential Rector of St Fagan's, and after leaving Cheltenham College, David had become a leading player with the South Wales Cricket Club and also captained St Fagan's from the early 1880s until 1899. He also regularly accepted invitations to field an eleven, under his leadership, in country house matches. David served on the Glamorgan committee until 1907, and acted as land agent for the Margam Estate, on whose property he helped to oversee the creation of the Margam cricket pitch.

Dai Davies

RHB and RM or OB, 1923-1939

Born: Llanelli, 26 August 1896
Died: Llanelli, 16 July 1976

Batting career:

M	I	NO	Runs	Av
411	681	61	15008	24.20

50	100	CT/ST
71	16	193

Bowling career:

O	M	R	W	Av
3661.4	774	9404	271	34.70

5wI	10wM
4	–

Career best performances:
216 v Somerset, Newport, 1939
6/50 v Essex, Westcliff, 1936

Dai Davies was Glamorgan's first home-bred professional to make an impact in County Championship cricket. During a playing career from 1923 to 1939, the Llanelli-born all-rounder scored 15,008 runs, and when he retired his aggregate was the highest in the club's history. Davies was also a useful off-spinner, having also bowled seam in his youth. During his career, he took 271 wickets, besides holding 193 catches, and was described by Jack Hobbs as the finest cover point he ever saw.

Dai initially played Minor County cricket for his native Carmarthenshire after the Great War and was employed in a steelworks at Llanelli. His fine all-round performances drew the attention of the Glamorgan selectors, who were keen to blood local talent at county level. Dai's chance came in 1923 and his home debut amazingly followed a double nightshift and a hectic car journey to Swansea. As befitted a steelworker, Dai was never afraid of hard work, and over the next sixteen years he became one of the county's most consistent and reliable batsman, hitting three consecutive hundreds in 1928, including

165* against Sussex at Eastbourne, and winning selection for the end of season encounter between the Players and the Gentlemen.

Davies's best season with the bat was in 1930, during which he aggregated 1,475 runs, with a century against Warwickshire and 11 half-centuries. Davies played one of his most memorable innings in 1932, during the match with Nottinghamshire at the Arms Park, as he hit 106 and shared a stand of 220 for the third wicket with Maurice Turnbull as the visiting bowlers experimented with the new technique of 'bodyline' bowling.

Davies only played in the opening three matches of 1934 after a stomach ulcer haemorrhaged during the match against Kent. He spent over a fortnight in hospital in Gravesend and missed the rest of the season, but he returned to the side in 1935 and continued to be a dependable run-scorer. Indeed, in 1939 he scored a career best double hundred during an ill-tempered match with Somerset at Newport. The Glamorgan players had been annoyed by the visitors slow play on

Dai Davies (extreme left) with fellow umpire Frank Lee and the England team led by Len Hutton at The Oval in 1953, after they had beaten Australia to win the Ashes.

the first day, so when they prolonged their innings into the second day, Maurice Turnbull told his batsmen to stay out in the middle for the rest of the game. At the same time, there was a strike at Bedwas Colliery and Dai Davies decided to show his sympathy with the miners by occupying the crease for as long as possible. Before going out to resume his innings on the final morning, he told Emrys Davies to wave to him when the Bedwas strike was over. Eventually, news reached the Rodney Parade ground that the miners were back at work, so Emrys duly waved to Dai – he promptly went down the wicket to a Somerset spinner and was stumped for 216!

After the Second World War, Davies became a first-class umpire and stood in 23 Tests between 1947 and 1958. He was also standing in the match at Bournemouth in 1948 when Glamorgan defeated Hampshire to win the Championship for the first time. Legend has it that when Dai raised his finger to adjudge the last Hampshire man leg before wicket, he said 'that's out and we've won the Championship!'

A cigarette card featuring Dai Davies.

Emrys Davies

LHB and SLA, 1924-1954

Born: Sandy, Carms., 27 June 1904
Died: Llanelli, 10 November, 1975

Batting career:

M	I	NO	Runs	Av
612	1016	79	26102	27.85

50	100	CT/ST
148	31	211

Bowling career:

O	M	R	W	Av
10263.4	2359	26030	885	29.41

5wI	10wM
32	2

Career best performances:
287* v Gloucestershire, Newport, 1939
6/24 v Leicestershire, Newport, 1935

Emrys Davies gave yeoman service to Glamorgan in a career spanning thirty years, during which time the left-handed batsman and left-arm spinner set a host of county records, many of which still stand today, including the highest ever score for Glamorgan in first-class cricket with 287* against Gloucestershire at Newport in 1939. In his overall career, Davies scored 26,566 runs in all first-class games, hit 32 centuries and took a total of 903 wickets at an average of 29.26.

Born in Carmarthenshire in 1904, Davies made his Glamorgan debut in 1924 after some excellent performances for Llanelli CC and the West Wales county. However, his early years with Glamorgan were quite modest ones and there were calls for his contract to be terminated. However, Johnnie Clay was of the opinion that Davies had a sound enough batting technique to make the grade, and all that was needed was greater experience and confidence. Maurice Turnbull agreed and they continued to support Davies, who eventually hit a maiden century against Essex at the Arms Park in 1932.

As Clay had believed, this proved to be the turning point in Davies's career and the left-hander moved up to open the batting with Arnold Dyson. Their partnership, until 1947, proved to be amongst the most successful in Glamorgan's history and Davies proved that his nickname of 'The Rock' was a most fitting one. Emrys also passed the 1,000 run mark for the first time in his career in 1932 and he proceeded to pass it every season for the next fifteen summers. In fact, on six occasions he passed 1,500 runs, with his most productive season being 1937, when Davies compiled 1,954 runs with centuries against Leicestershire, Warwickshire and Sussex.

He also developed into a fine spin bowler, filling the gap in the county's attack following the release of Frank Ryan on financial grounds. Davies proved a perfect foil to Johnnie Clay and in 1935 Emrys became the first Glamorgan player to achieve the double of 1,000 runs and 100 wickets, whilst in 1937 he scored a century and took a hat-trick against Leicestershire at Leicester.

Emrys's finest innings for Glamorgan came at Newport in 1939, when he occupied the crease

Emrys Davies, nicknamed 'The Rock', carefully watches a delivery in the early 1950s.

for seven and a half hours whilst making an unbeaten 287 against Gloucestershire. This is still the highest individual score in the county's history and Davies might have been the first to score a triple hundred had the Gloucestershire captain not placed all of his fielders on the boundary towards the end of Davies's marathon innings.

He was no less effective after the Second World War and in 1947, at the age of forty-three, Emrys created a new club record with five centuries during the summer. In all, he hit 1,615 runs, yet the veteran still managed to better that in 1948, when he amassed 1,708 first-class runs, scoring 215 against Essex at Brentwood during a record partnership of 313 with Willie Jones. It was fitting that the stalwart opener should finish that marvellous summer of 1948 as the club's leading run scorer, and time and again he carefully laid the foundation of the Glamorgan innings.

His all-round abilities had been acknowledged by the England selectors, who included him on the 1939/40 MCC tour to India. However, almost as soon as Emrys had started to think about the prospect of playing for England, war was declared and the tour was cancelled. However, Davies was not robbed of the opportunity of participating in Test cricket, as after retiring from playing in 1954, he became one of the country's top umpires and stood in 9 Tests from 1956 until 1959. One of these games was the famous Test at Old Trafford when Jim Laker took 19 wickets for 90 runs against Australia in 1956.

Emrys also spent many years coaching at Llandovery College, besides spending his winters in Johannesburg, where many South African schoolboys benefited from his wise advice and vast experience. Indeed, Alan Melville, the South African captain and selector, considered Davies to have been one of the finest coaches of his generation. Davies was also a devout Christian and often put his faith before cricket. Many of his contemporaries believe that it was this spiritual strength and the goodness in his heart, which allowed Emrys to keep on playing county cricket until the age of fifty.

Haydn Davies

RHB and WK, 1935-1958

Born: Llanelli, 23 April 1919
Died: Haverfordwest, 4 September 1993
Batting career:

M	I	NO	Runs	Av
423	596	95	6515	13.00

50	100	CT/ST
11	–	581/203

Bowling career:

O	M	R	W	Av
3.0	0	20	1	20.00

5wI	10wM
–	–

Career best performances:
80 v South Africans, Arms Park, 1951
1/20 v Nottinghamshire, Trent Bridge, 1951

Haydn Davies is regarded by many players and long time supporters of Glamorgan CCC to have been the finest wicketkeeper ever to represent the Welsh county and, even in the twilight of his career in 1955, he took a record 8 dismissals against the South Africans at Swansea.

He was also one of the best 'keepers never to have won Test honours; the nearest he got to higher recognition was selection in the 1946 Test trial. Davies was unfortunate enough to be at the peak of his career at the same time as Godfrey Evans and the England selectors regularly preferred the wicketkeeper from Kent.

Davies joined the Glamorgan staff in 1934 after graduating from Aberystwyth University. He made his county debut in 1935, playing initially as a specialist batsman and swift runner in the outfield. His immense promise behind the stumps was recognised in 1938 as he took over on a regular basis from Tom Brierley. After the interruption of the Second World War, he played in every Championship match between 1947 and 1957, often playing with broken fingers strapped and bandaged. His swift glovework impressed many people and some writers believe that during this time he was the best exponent of leg-side stumpings in county cricket.

He was a technically correct batsman and on five occasions passed 500 runs for the season. Despite having spent hours behind the stumps, he was always prepared to act as an emergency opening batsman or the role of nightwatchman if wickets fell shortly before the close of play. On his day, Davies could be an explosive hitter and he struck a career best 80 in his benefit match against the 1951 South Africans.

His high quality wicketkeeping and penchant for hitting sixes made him a very popular figure with Glamorgan's supporters. Indeed, amongst the highlights of Glamorgan's performance in the field would be Haydn's vociferous appealing or his joyful and deft stumpings as opponents completely misread the spin of Clay, Muncer, McConnon and Shepherd.

Despite a heavy build, Davies was an excellent squash player and, after retiring in 1958, he became the professional at the Edinburgh Squash and Tennis Club.

Born: Cardiff, 1 January 1946

Batting career:

M	I	NO	Runs	Av
213	369	30	7363	21.71
121	*107*	*8*	*1629*	*16.45*

50	100	CT/ST
35	5	208
6	*–*	*41*

Bowling career:

O	M	R	W	Av
2868.0	700	7793	241	32.33
475.1	*48*	*1941*	*70*	*27.73*

5wI	10wM
6	–

Career best performances:
134 v Worcestershire, Sophia Gardens, 1971
6/62 v Gloucestershire, Cheltenham, 1970
91 v Northants, Wellingborough, 1975
4/48 v Essex, Swansea, 1969

For a few awful moments during Glamorgan's Championship match with Warwickshire at Cardiff in 1971, it looked as if Roger Davis would not recover from being hit a sickening blow on the side of his head whilst fielding at short-leg. As soon as he was hit, Davis collapsed, went into convulsions and had to be given the kiss of life by a doctor who ran onto the Sophia Gardens ground from the members' enclosure. Thankfully, this helped to save Davis's life and he fully recovered. By the following season he was back as a regular in the Glamorgan side.

The former Blundell's schoolboy had made his county debut in 1964, and he developed into a sound and cool headed middle-order batsman, and accurate off-spin bowler. Later in his career, Roger moved up to open the batting with Alan Jones and in 1975 he enjoyed his most profitable season, amassing 1,243 runs, with centuries against Leicestershire and Sussex.

Davis was also a handy player in one-day matches. His finest innings came in 1973, as he hit 101 against the West Indies in their Sunday friendly at Swansea. Glamorgan had been set a target of 248 in 39 overs and Davis shared a blistering opening partnership of 129 with Alan Jones. He subsequently received useful support from Mike Llewellyn, but their sterling efforts were ultimately in vain as Glamorgan fell nine runs short of their target.

Despite his near fatal accident, Davis was a brilliant fielder close to the wicket – and this was in the days when the only protection a fielder wore was a box – and stood fearlessly close to batsmen, taking many fine catches off the spin bowling of Don Shepherd. He rarely missed a chance and his 33 catches during 1969 was one of the vital ingredients in Glamorgan winning the County Championship for the second time in the club's history.

Davis lost form in 1976 and it was a huge surprise when the club opted to dispense with his services at the end of the season without a benefit after thirteen years of service to the county. Despite his abrupt release, Davis has acted in recent years on the Glamorgan committee, and his older brother John also played for Glamorgan between 1959 and 1967.

Winston Davis
RHB and RFM, 1982-1984

Born: St Vincent, 18 September 1958

Batting career:

M	I	NO	Runs	Av
45	51	21	471	15.70
31	*11*	*4*	*32*	*4.57*

50	100	CT/ST
1	–	14
–	–	9

Bowling career:

O	M	R	W	Av
1315.2	285	4211	142	29.65
235.5	*26*	*927*	*43*	*21.56*

5wI	10wM
6	–

Career best performances:
50 v Nottinghamshire, Trent Bridge, 1984
7/70 v Nottinghamshire, Ebbw Vale, 1983
8 v Somerset, Swansea, 1984
5/29 v Middlesex, Sophia Gardens, 1984

With 142 first-class wickets to his name for Glamorgan between 1982 and 1984, Winston Davis holds the record as the most successful overseas bowler in the club's history. Tragedy has, however, struck the pace bowler in the past few years, as he is now paralysed after having fallen in an accident whilst clearing trees in his native West Indies.

Davis joined Glamorgan in 1982, after Ezra Moseley sustained a stress fracture, and he responded with 42 wickets in his 13 first-class appearances, despite being plagued by run-up problems and a tendency to deliver no-balls. He took a further 52 wickets at 26 apiece in 1983, and his tally could have been higher had he not been in the West Indian party for the World Cup. Indeed, the lithe and whippy fast bowler enjoyed a successful tournament, during which he took 7/51 against Australia at Headingley to produce the best ever figures in the competition.

Davis was surprisingly omitted from the West Indian party to tour England in 1984, so he returned to Glamorgan at the start of the season. However, after an injury to Milton Small, Davis was summoned into the tour party and ended up top of the bowling averages. Davis took 14 first-class wickets at 14 apiece, largely as a result of returns of 5/32 and 5/39 against Derbyshire. He also produced a career best 77 in the Old Trafford Test, after coming in as a nightwatchman.

Davis's efforts on the England tour resulted in his inclusion in the West Indian party that toured Australia in 1984/85, but they were not sufficient to earn an extension to his contract with Glamorgan. Indeed, the county's committee were faced at the end of the 1984 season with the difficult decision of choosing between Davis's raw pace or the brilliant batting of Javed Miandad. The committee opted for the Pakistani maestro and Davis later joined Northamptonshire in 1987. He played for the East Midlands county until 1990 and returned career best figures of 7/52 for Northamptonshire against Sussex at Northampton in 1988.

Davis played first-class cricket for Wellington and Tasmania, captained the Windward Islands in 1988, and appeared in 15 Tests and 35 one-day internationals for the West Indies.

Dick Duckfield
RHB and RM, 1930-1938

Born: Maesteg, 2 July 1907
Died: Bridgend, 30 December 1959
Batting career:

M	I	NO	Runs	Av
191	301	39	6894	26.31

50	100	CT/ST
37	9	26

Bowling career:

O	M	R	W	Av
53.0	1	255	0	–

5wI	10wM
–	–

Career best performance:
280* v Surrey, The Oval, 1936

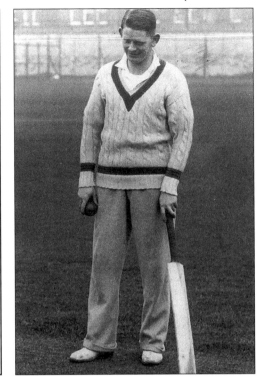

Dick Duckfield established a Glamorgan batting record in 1936 by hitting an unbeaten 280 against Surrey at The Oval. At the time it was a new club record for the highest individual innings in the club's history and a very bright future was predicted for the Maesteg-born batsman. Yet within two years Duckfield had retired from the county game after a complete loss of confidence.

Duckfield had made his Glamorgan debut in 1930 and in 1932 the right-handed batsman secured a regular place in the county's middle order. In 1933 he scored his maiden first-class hundred in the august surroundings of Lord's Cricket Ground, hitting an elegant 121 against Middlesex. Duckfield also passed 1,000 runs for the first time in his career in 1933, hitting a total of 1,343 runs, which included centuries against Gloucestershire and Leicestershire. He consolidated on this headway in 1934 with two further centuries, against Kent and Cambridge University, and during the season was also selected to play for the Players against the Gentlemen.

Duckfield's finest hour for Glamorgan came at The Oval in June 1936. During his marathon five and a half hour innings against Surrey, Duckfield struck a record 39 fours, and shared in two sizeable partnerships. He put on 181 for the fourth wicket with Tom Brierley and added 186 for the sixth wicket with Dai Davies. In the second innings, Duckfield made a rapid half-century to take his match aggregate to 330 without being dismissed. This still remains the only time a Glamorgan player has scored over 300 runs during the course of a match.

His efforts showed that Duckfield had the temperament to compile large innings, but soon afterwards he started to doubt his ability in the field and he found it increasingly difficult to either catch a ball in the air or field a ball running along the ground. As this started to play on his mind, Duckfield also lost form with the bat and consequently lost his place in the county's side. His problems sadly resulted in his retirement from professional cricket at the end of the 1938 season, although he did reappear in Glamorgan's fund-raising friendlies during 1944.

Arnold Dyson
RHB and RM, 1926-1949

Born: Halifax, 10 July 1905
Died: Goldsborough, 7 June 1978

Batting career:

M	I	NO	Runs	Av
412	696	37	17920	27.19

50	100	CT/ST
92	24	243/1

Bowling career:

O	M	R	W	Av
34.0	2	160	1	160.00

5wI	10wM
–	–

Career best performances:
208 v Surrey, The Oval, 1932
1/9 v Lancashire, Old Trafford, 1938

Arnold Dyson holds the record for 305 consecutive appearances in Championship cricket between 1930 and 1947 – a fine tribute to both his fitness and his consistency with the bat. Indeed, during this period the steady opening batsman formed a most productive partnership with Emrys Davies. The Dyson-Davies combination became known as 'The Old Firm' and is still amongst the most successful in the club's history, with the pair sharing no less than 32 century partnerships.

The right-handed batsman and occasional wicketkeeper had moved from his native Yorkshire to South Wales during the mid-1920s, having failed to secure a place on the county's staff. He subsequently qualified for the Welsh county by playing in the South Wales Cricket Association for Neath CC and made his Glamorgan debut in 1926.

An engineer by profession, Dyson applied the same calculating mind to his batting, carefully reducing the number of loose strokes in his repertoire. Dyson's neat style and agile fielding won him a regular place in the Glamorgan side and he quickly developed into one of the most reliable opening batsmen on the county circuit, hitting a career best double century against Surrey in 1932. Whilst Dyson could always be relied upon to play the anchor role in Glamorgan's batting, he could also be a fast scorer, as indicated by his century before lunch against Kent in 1937.

He combined both grit and grace to pass 1,000 runs in every season from 1931 until 1947, with the exception of 1936 when he fell 65 runs short of the target after a loss of form in July. Dyson's most productive season was in 1938, when he chalked up 1,885 runs and struck centuries against Hampshire, Sussex, Cambridge University and also Sir Julian Cahn's XI, with whom he toured New Zealand in 1938/39.

He took a well-earned benefit in 1939, followed by a testimonial in the Championship winning season of 1948, during which Dyson made his final appearance for his adopted county. After the Second World War, Dyson coached at Oundle School.

David Evans
RHB and WK, 1956-1969

Born: Lambeth, 27 July 1933
Died: Llandyssul, 25 March 1990

Batting career:

M	I	NO	Runs	Av
270	364	91	2875	10.53
5	2	0	9	4.50

50	100	CT/ST
–	–	503/55
–	–	6

Bowling career:

O	M	R	W	Av
4.0	0	12	0	–

5wI	10wM
–	–

Career best performances:
46* v Oxford University, Oxford, 1961
8 v Surrey, The Oval, 1965

David Evans was one of the best and most unobtrusive wicketkeepers in county cricket during the mid-1960s, and he retired in 1969 with 558 dismissals to his name. According to some, Evans might have won Test honours if he had been a more flamboyant 'keeper.

Evans was brought up near Ammanford and joined the Glamorgan staff during the mid-1950s as understudy to Haydn Davies. He made his first-class debut in 1956 and took over behind the stumps on a regular basis after Davies had retired at the end of the 1958 season. Evans continued the high standards which Davies had set and he deservedly won his county cap in 1959 after some excellent performances behind the stumps, both standing up to the spinners and standing back to the quicker bowlers.

Evans spent many hours in the nets developing his technique and whilst Glamorgan were batting, Evans would quietly sit in the pavilion, closely studying the method of his opposite number. His patience and diligence paid off as he made 79 dismissals in 1961 and 82 in 1962, before claiming 89 victims in 1963 to beat Haydn Davies's county record. Evans sustained a back injury during 1964 and temporarily lost his place to Eifion Jones. He regained his fitness and his place in 1965, and in 1967 he took six catches in an innings against Yorkshire to equal another one of Davies's club records. Evans could have broken the record, as he got his fingertips to a seventh chance, and unselfishly let another fielder catch a top edge which Evans could easily have run underneath.

With the Welsh county needing to bolster their batting, preference was given to Eifion Jones from 1968. Despite the bitter disappointment of losing his place, Evans gracefully played on a regular basis for the county's Second XI and helped Phil Clift groom the junior players. Evans took a benefit in 1969, before retiring and becoming a first-class umpire in 1971. He brought to his new job the same high qualities and drive for perfection that he had shown behind the stumps for the Welsh county. He stood in 9 Test matches between 1981 and 1985, including the famous Test between England and Australia at Headingley in 1981.

Trevor Every
RHB and WK, 1929-1934

Born: Llanelli, 19 December 1909
Died: Newport, 20 January 1990
Batting career:

M	I	NO	Runs	Av
128	198	44	2518	18.35

50	100	CT/ST
8	1	108/70

Bowling career:

O	M	R	W	Av
8.0	0	49	0	–

5wI	10wM
–	–

Career best performance:
116 v Worcestershire, Stourbridge, 1932

Some might scoff at Every's inclusion in this book, given that he only played for the county from 1929 until 1934. However, had he not lost his sight and been forced into premature retirement, Trevor Every might have been one of the finest batsmen/wicketkeepers in the club's history. During his short career, Every claimed 108 catches and 70 stumpings, as well as scoring 2,518 runs in 128 matches.

Trevor Every showed rich promise as a schoolboy cricketer, keeping wicket for Llanelli club in the newly created South Wales Cricket Association. With Glamorgan looking to sign up promising locally-born players, it was not long before the name of T. Every entered the notebooks of the club's talent scouts.

He joined the county's staff on leaving school in 1928 and the following year he made his Championship debut against Yorkshire at the Arms Park. He soon won a regular place in the side and established himself as one of the best young 'keepers on the county circuit. He took 47 dismissals in 1930 and again in 1932, and his haul would have been twice this amount had Glamorgan not suffered a series of heavy defeats by an innings. Every also developed into a gritty lower middle-order batsman, making three half-centuries in 1930 and 1931, before hitting 116 against Worcestershire at Stourbridge in 1932, striking thirteen crisp fours, and sharing a useful eighth-wicket partnership over an hour and a half with Dick Duckfield.

Many good judges were forecasting a bright future for the young wicketkeeper, but in 1934 he developed eye problems in the pre-season practices. By the opening game of the season against Kent at the Arms Park, Trevor was finding it difficult to pick up the flight of the ball and, midway through the game, he was taken to consult an eye specialist. He told Trevor the devastating news that he was going blind and Every never played another game for Glamorgan. Indeed, the scorebook for the second innings of the match with Kent simply records Trevor as being 'absent ill'. By the end of the summer, Trevor had completely lost his sight. Over the winter months of 1934/35 he started training as a stenographer with the RNIB in Cardiff.

Roy Fredericks

LHB and SLA, 1971-1973

Born: British Guyana, 11 November 1942

Batting career:

M	I	NO	Runs	Av
45	80	8	2991	41.54
45	*45*	*0*	*1047*	*23.27*

50	100	CT/ST
12	7	21
7	–	24

Bowling career:

O	M	R	W	Av
207.1	45	667	20	33.35
6.5	*0*	*35*	*1*	*35.00*

5wI	10wM
–	–

Career best performances:
228* v Northamptonshire, Swansea, 1972
3/37 v Northamptonshire, Swansea, 1971
87 v Hampshire, Bournemouth, 1972
1/17 v Nottinghamshire, Trent Bridge, 1971

Roy Fredericks was Glamorgan's first overseas Test player from the Caribbean. The Guyanese left-hander made his Test debut on the West Indies tour to Australia in 1968/69 and he made a very favourable impression during their tour to England in 1969. Fredericks joined Glamorgan in 1971 and, during his first season in county cricket, the West Indian emerged as a tough and hard-hitting opener, amassing 1,377 runs.

He began his Glamorgan career with innings of 66 and 145* against Nottinghamshire at Trent Bridge, and throughout the season displayed an adventurous (and at times somewhat unorthodox) approach to opening the batting. Whilst this was sometimes his undoing in Championship matches, he often flourished in the one-day games and delighted the Welsh crowds with his cavalier strokeplay. One example of this came in the Sunday League match at Swansea against Yorkshire where Fredericks hit a blistering 84 off just 88 deliveries, hitting 7 sixes and 8 fours with some fierce drives and savage pulls against the Yorkshire bowlers.

After a modest start to 1972, Fredericks struck a rich vein of form in the second half of the season, hitting 228* against Northamptonshire at Swansea and sharing a record opening partnership of 330 with Alan Jones. He followed this with 126 in the next match against Middlesex and took his aggregate in his final six innings of 1972 to 615 runs at an average of 123.

He only made a handful of appearances during 1973, as he was a member of the West Indian tour party competing in the Test series with England. In fact, this proved to be his final summer with the Welsh county, as Glamorgan decided to seek an overseas pace bowler instead to spearhead their bowling attack.

Fredericks continued to play Test cricket for the West Indies and in 1975 was in their team which won the inaugural World Cup. He later joined the World Series Cricket team in Australia in 1977/78 and continued playing for Guyana until retiring at the end of the 1982/83 season. He has since served as Minister of Sport in Guyana and become a West Indian selector.

Roy Gabe-Jones
RHB and RM, 1922

Born: Clydach Vale, 25 November 1906
Died: Cardiff, 26 February 1965

Batting career:

M	I	NO	Runs	Av
1	1	1	6	–

50	100	CT/ST
–	–	–

Career best performance:
6* v Leicestershire, Arms Park, 1922

Roy Gabe-Jones richly deserves inclusion in any book celebrating the deeds of the county's players as, in 1922, he became the youngest county cricketer of the twentieth century when he made his County Championship debut against Leicestershire at Cardiff Arms Park in 1922, aged just fifteen years and nine months old.

Born at Clydach Vale in 1906, Gabe-Jones was educated at Blundell's School in Tiverton, where he showed great promise as a sportsman, playing rugby and cricket for his school. Each summer, he returned to South Wales, and during the summer holidays of 1922 was playing as usual for Clydach Vale CC with few thoughts of ever playing county cricket, never mind during that very summer.

After a string of good scores he was included in a Glamorgan Colts game in early August, and his steady batting and outstanding fielding impressed the watching county selectors. They were keen to improve the fielding of their team, many of whom were on the wrong side of thirty, so when several players dropped out for the final game of the season, Gabe-Jones was drafted in to make a remarkable debut. The schoolboy made a stubborn 6* against the Leicestershire bowlers and helped the depleted Glamorgan side to secure a draw.

His obdurate batting and splendid ground fielding drew praise from the spectators and press alike, and some of the watching journalists penned articles about the county's new 'boy wonder'! Yet despite such a fine debut this was, remarkably, his only first-class appearance. After leading the Blundell's First XI and attending Cambridge University, Gabe-Jones went into business in Cardiff. He played rugby for Cardiff RFC and continued to play club cricket in the Cardiff area as well as turning out for the county's second eleven and in exhibition matches. Nevertheless, he has retained a special place in the club's history as nobody has ever beaten his remarkable record of being the county's youngest ever player.

Born: Worcester, 19 July 1911
Died: Cardiff, 23 March 1967

Batting career:

M	I	NO	Runs	Av
47	73	23	406	8.12

50	100	CT/ST
1	–	18

Bowling career:

O	M	R	W	Av
1207.5	175	4284	118	36.60

5wI	10wM
3	–

Career best performances:
62 v Somerset, Downside School, 1934
5/79 v Northamptonshire, Kettering, 1935

Ted Glover was typical of the colourful and jovial amateurs who willingly played for Glamorgan during the 1930s. Glover was a useful all-round sportsman, playing cricket for Glamorgan CCC and rugby for Glamorgan Wanderers RFC. He was also an influential sports journalist and, after retiring from county cricket, he helped to promote the game in the post-war era by editing *The South Wales Cricketers' Magazine*. This publication gave greater prominence to club cricket and amongst the articles were those giving coaching advice to young cricketers.

Educated at Sherborne School, Glover played for the Lord's Schools against The Rest in 1929, before making his first-class debut for Glamorgan in 1932 against India at Cardiff Arms Park. He was a useful fast-medium bowler and in 1935 returned figures of 5/79 against Northamptonshire at Kettering, followed by 5/95 against Kent at Cardiff Arms Park. His work commitments often restricted his appearances, but he proved to be a hostile seam bowler both at county level and in club cricket. In the case of the latter, one of his best performances came in 1934 when he took 7/38 for Cardiff CC against the powerful Neath CC.

Glover was also a bold and aggressive tail-end batsman who played a number of entertaining innings at club level, as well as scoring a rapid half-century for Glamorgan against Somerset at Downside School in 1934 during a tenth-wicket partnership of 70 with his friend Johnnie Clay. During the course of his career best 62, Glover struck 4 sixes and 4 fours, and then went out to take 5/88 as Glamorgan, largely through Glover's efforts, secured a handsome first innings lead.

Given different circumstances, Glover could easily have become a highly successful professional cricketer. He was also the brother-in-law of Glamorgan captain Maurice Turnbull, who lost his life during the Second World War. However, Glover continued his good friend's work by promoting the cause of Glamorgan CCC in newspapers and magazines.

Rt Hon. Lord Justice Hugh Griffiths MC

RHB and RFM, 1946-1948

Born: Marylebone, 26 September 1923

Batting career:

M	I	NO	Runs	Av
8	11	2	34	3.77

50	100	CT/ST
–	–	–

Bowling career:

O	M	R	W	Av
173.3	30	538	17	31.64

5wI	10wM
–	–

Career best performances:

12 v Gloucestershire, Cheltenham, 1947
4/61 v Surrey, Arms Park, 1947

The Right Honourable Lord Justice Griffiths only had a brief career as a fast bowler with Glamorgan after the Second World War, but he has subsequently had a most distinguished career in the legal world as a Life Peer and a Law Lord. He still retained an interest in cricket and acted as president of the MCC during 1990/91, thereby becoming the first Glamorgan player to achieve this honour with the most famous cricket club in the world.

Educated at Charterhouse, Hugh Griffiths was in the school's XI in 1940 and 1941, before serving in the Second World War and being awarded the Military Cross for bravely disarming a tank. After the war ended, Griffiths went to St John's, Cambridge, to commence his legal studies. However, he also found time to win Blues in 1946, 1947 and 1948, during which time he recorded career best figures of 6/129 against Lancashire at Fenner's in 1946, besides scoring 19 in the 1948 Varsity match at Lord's.

It was whilst he was a student at Cambridge that Griffiths played for Glamorgan during his summer vacations. He made his county debut in 1946 when Peter Judge was injured for the match against Kent at Dover. Griffiths took 4/64 in his first appearance and was called up again in August 1947, when the young quick bowler took 4/61 against a strong Surrey side. He also made four further appearances during July and August 1948 as Wilf Wooller rotated his bowling resources, depending on the nature of the wickets. As it turned out, all of Griffiths's games in the Championship winning season of 1948 were on away soil, as he played at Northampton, Hull, Edgbaston and Leicester.

After leaving Cambridge, he pursued a highly successful legal career, culminating in his elevation to a High Court Judge, and he also gave judgement in the famous 'Spycatcher' case during the 1980s.

Bernard Hedges

RHB, 1950-1967

Born: Pontypridd, 10 November 1927

Batting career:

M	I	NO	Runs	Av
422	744	41	17733	25.22
7	*7*	*1*	*250*	*41.67*

50	100	CT/ST
84	21	200
1	*1*	*4*

Bowling career:

O	M	R	W	Av
94.0	24	260	3	86.67
38.0	*13*	*134*	*8*	*16.75*

5wI	10wM
–	–

Career best performances:
182 v Oxford University, Oxford, 1967
1/16 v Oxford University, Oxford, 1967
103 v Somerset, Arms Park, 1963
2/17 v Somerset, Arms Park, 1963

Bernard Hedges had an eighteen-year career with Glamorgan, during which he amassed over 17,000 runs in first-class cricket and scored the county's first ever century in limited-overs cricket, with 103 against Somerset at the Arms Park in 1963. During his career, Hedges struck 21 centuries in first-class cricket, including a Championship best 141 against Kent at Swansea in 1961, as well as 144 against the 1962 Pakistanis at the Arms Park.

The Pontypridd-born batsman had joined the Glamorgan staff in 1950 after completing his National Service. Indeed, during his duties with the RAF, he hit a well-made 143 against the Minor Counties in 1948. Hedges played initially in Glamorgan's middle-order, before moving up to open the batting in the late 1950s. His sound technique, wide array of strokes and steadfast temperament all allowed Hedges to become a heavy run-scorer in Championship cricket. Hedges's quick eye and nimble footwork also meant that he was amongst the county's best players of spin bowling.

Wilf Wooller once wrote that Hedges was 'swift of foot and quick of eye' and 'the best player of slow spin bowling in Glamorgan since the war. No player has been more at ease on the awkward turning wickets. He is happy cutting the leg-spinner square, stroking away the off-spinner with the spin into midfield, never with great power, the rapier rather than the broadsword was his weapon.' Many regard his finest innings to have been the 139 he made against Nottinghamshire on a turning wicket at Stradey Park, Llanelli, when he deftly mastered the wiles of Australian leg-spinner Bruce Dooland.

Hedges also had a keen sense of fair play and would often walk after the faintest of edges, sometimes even turning for the pavilion before the fielders had appealed – not for him the modern habit of standing until the umpire's finger is raised. Instead, Hedges would simply return to the dressing rooms and, if any of his colleagues asked him why he did not wait, Hedges would modestly tell them 'I was out, man. That's all there is to it!'

David Hemp
LHB and RM, 1991-1996

Born: Bermuda, 8 November 1970

Batting career:

M	I	NO	Runs	Av
71	124	11	3662	32.41
60	*47*	*2*	*974*	*21.64*

50	100	CT/ST
21	6	48
5	*1*	*27*

Bowling Career:

O	M	R	W	Av
63.0	5	330	10	33.00
6.2	*0*	*43*	*1*	*43.00*

5wI	10wM
–	–

Career best performances:
157 v Gloucestershire, Abergavenny, 1995
3/23 v South Africa 'A', Sophia Gardens, 1996
121 v Combined Univs, Sophia Gardens, 1995
1/14 v Leicestershire, Swansea, 1996

David Hemp was an elegant and graceful strokemaker with Glamorgan between 1991 and 1996, before joining Warwickshire in 1997. His classical strokeplay was based upon a sound technique and, from an early age, the former Millfield schoolboy showed an ability to play long innings. Indeed, the left-hander scored four consecutive centuries for Welsh Schools in 1990 and the following season hit an unbeaten 258 for Wales against the MCC.

Hemp made his first Glamorgan appearance in August 1991 during Glamorgan's Sunday League fixture against Surrey at The Oval and the following year he established a place in the county's middle order. In 1993 he was a member of the Glamorgan team that won the Sunday League title. He recorded his maiden Championship hundred against Warwickshire at Edgbaston in 1994 and consolidated on this progress with three further centuries that summer, during which he amassed 1,452 runs, and deservedly won a place on the England 'A' tour to India and Bangladesh in 1994/95.

This was perhaps the high point in his career with Glamorgan, as 1995 was a quite modest season for the Bermuda-born batsman. Despite making a career best 157 against Gloucestershire at Abergavenny, Hemp struggled for consistency. Then, early in the 1996 season, Hemp sustained two broken ribs and damaged his lungs after colliding with Hugh Morris whilst attempting to field the ball against the Combined Universities at Cambridge at the end of April. He spent several weeks on the sidelines before regaining his place in the Glamorgan side, taking a career best 3/23 with his medium-pace bowling against South Africa 'A' at Cardiff.

At the end of that summer, Hemp agreed terms with Warwickshire, where he has regained form and become a cultured run-maker at number three. In 1997 he scored three centuries in four innings, with 138 and 114* against Hampshire, followed by 117 in the second innings of the match against Kent. In 1999 he added two further centuries to his tally, with 144 in Warwickshire's victory over Worcestershire, and then 100 on a lively Trent Bridge wicket when Nottinghamshire were beaten by 55 runs.

Born: Marylebone, 17 December 1924
Died: Oxford, 11 September 1987

Batting career:

M	I	NO	Runs	Av
133	166	74	869	9.45

50	100	CT/ST
–	–	60

Bowling Career:

O	M	R	W	Av
3138.0	629	7400	318	23.27

5wI	10wM
11	–

Career best performances:
40 v Leicestershire, Leicester, 1950
7/55 v Hampshire, Swansea, 1952

Norman Hever was Glamorgan's strike bowler during their Championship winning summer of 1948. During the season his lively fast-medium bowling claimed 84 wickets at just 17 apiece. It was a sterling performance that deservedly brought Hever both his county cap and selection in the 1949 Test trial at Edgbaston.

'Pete' Hever had initially been on the MCC groundstaff and played a handful of games for Middlesex in 1947. He made an impressive debut for them, taking 5/26 in 13.1 overs against Hampshire, clean bowling four of the opposing batsmen. However, with many good bowlers at their disposal, Middlesex could not guarantee regular first team cricket for Hever and, with Glamorgan's Peter Judge struggling for fitness, he joined the Welsh county in 1948.

Hever made an immediate impact for his new employers when, during his first two seasons with Glamorgan, he took 154 wickets and was cleverly used by captain Wilf Wooller in short and very effective bursts.

Amongst his returns in Championship cricket were 5/39 against Middlesex at the Arms Park and then 5/34 when the sides met at Lord's. He was a consistent wicket-taker during 1948, failing to take a wicket in just 1 of the 25 matches in which he bowled.

In 1949 Hever took 70 wickets, followed by a further 57 in 1950, as well as 63 in 1952. His role as a shock bowler meant that he never took 10 wickets in a match, but he still took 5 wickets in an innings on 11 occasions. Hever retired from county cricket in 1954 and, after a short spell in Welsh club cricket, he became groundsman at Peterborough and subsequently Northampton, where he worked from 1961 until 1973. A measure of his skill at preparing a wicket was that he won the Groundsman of the Year award on five occasions, including a consecutive run from 1982 until 1985. He also assisted with the coaching at the Wantage Road ground and amongst one of the players to benefit from his advice was future England batsman Wayne Larkins.

Vernon Hill
LHB and RM, 1905

Born: Llandaff, 30 January 1871
Died: Weston-Super-Mare, 29 Sept. 1932
Batting career:

M	I	NO	Runs	Av
(5	9	0	46	5.11)

50	100	CT/ST
(–	–	2)

Bowling Career:

O	M	R	W	Av
(18.0	4	43	0	–)

5wI	10wM
(–	–)

Career best performance:
(10 v Monmouthshire, Arms Park, 1905)

Vernon Hill gained Blues at Oxford in 1892 and 1893, and won fame as a bold striker of the ball after a fine innings of 114 in the 1892 Varsity Match helped defeat Cambridge by five wickets. Coming in at number seven, the left-hander shared a partnership of 180 for the sixth wicket with M.R. Jardine. *Wisden's* correspondent recorded that 'Hill from the very start, hit with wholehearted vigour and a fine contempt for consequences – all after Hill had backed himself to score a hundred!

Hill also played county cricket for Somerset and established a name for himself as a batsman, frequently hitting the ball with tremendous power off the front foot. In fact, there are many stories of him nonchalantly driving the fiery professional bowlers out of the nets at Taunton. During his Somerset career, the extrovert Hill played many cavalier innings, including a career best 116 against Kent at Taunton in 1898.

Hill returned to his native South Wales around the turn of the century and took over the captaincy of Cardiff CC. He subsequently played a highly important role off the field for Glamorgan, helping his good friend Joseph Brain to stage a number of fund-raising fixtures at Cardiff to boost the county's finances. Hill also persuaded several well-known amateurs to turn out in these exhibition games and it was his idea that the county should stage an annual Gents versus Players match as part of a weekly festival at the Arms Park. As a result, the county reaped many social and financial benefits, and without the cash raised from these fixtures it is doubtful if Glamorgan would have been able to start their campaign in search of first-class status.

Hill made a handful of appearances in Minor County matches in 1905 for Glamorgan, although his best years were behind him and his contributions were quite modest. Even so, his classical and aggressive strokeplay was still evident in club cricket and Hill continued to scorer heavily for Cardiff and the MCC.

The son of Sir E.S. Hill of Llandaff, the Conservative MP for Bristol, he had a successful career as a lawyer. By the outbreak of the Great War, Hill had returned to the West Country. In 1930 he served as president of Somerset CCC.

Geoff Holmes
RHB and RM, 1978-1991

Born: Newcastle, 16 September 1958

Batting career:

M	I	NO	Runs	Av
203	325	50	7529	27.38
180	*164*	*30*	*3462*	*25.84*

50	100	CT/ST
34	9	82
18	*–*	*53*

Bowling career:

O	M	R	W	Av
1155.2	233	3963	88	45.03
700.2	*42*	*3389*	*133*	*25.48*

5wI	10wM
2	–

Career best performances:
125* Somerset, Sophia Gardens, 1990
5/38 v Essex, Colchester, 1988
73 v Warwickshire, Edgbaston, 1984
5/2 v Derbyshire, Ebbw Vale, 1984

Geoff Holmes was a most effective all-rounder for Glamorgan in limited-overs cricket in the 1980s. During the course of his career, Holmes returned some remarkable bowling figures, including 5/2 in the Sunday League match with Derbyshire at Ebbw Vale in 1984, as well as claiming a hat-trick at the same ground in 1987 in a fixture with Nottinghamshire.

The young Geordie was recommended to Glamorgan by Len Muncer, the MCC coach and former Glamorgan stalwart, after an impressive spell on the Lord's groundstaff in 1974. He duly confirmed his rich potential by scoring a century against Gloucestershire at Bristol after only a handful of innings in the Championship. It was an eventful innings in more ways than one for the young batsman, as during the course of his hundred he injured a shoulder, then had to face several interruptions from swarms of bees and reflecting car windscreens – and all whilst almost single-handedly fending off a series of bouncers from Gloucestershire fast bowler Mike Procter!

He subsequently developed into the typical all-rounder of the modern era – batting anywhere in the order from three to six, opening the batting in one-day games, bowling nagging medium pace, being a live wire in the field and running like a whippet between the wickets.

Holmes was an accumulator rather than a shot-a-ball batsman and his most productive season in Championship cricket was in 1985, when he amassed 1,129 runs and deservedly won his county cap. In 1988 he struck two hundreds in the game against Somerset at Taunton, 108 against the same opponents at Sophia Gardens and 117 against Gloucestershire at Bristol. Yet, despite these 4 hundreds, he ended up the season with 999 runs in first-class cricket, just one run short of passing 1,000 for the fourth time in his career. His efforts, however, were not lost on his fellow players and Glamorgan's supporters, who voted Holmes as Glamorgan's Player of the Year for 1988.

He also played and coached in South Africa and during 1989/1990 hit a career best 182 for Border against the Western Province 'B' side. A back injury forced Holmes to retire from county cricket at the end of 1991, his benefit season.

John Hopkins
RHB and occasional WK, 1970-1988

Born: Maesteg, 16 June 1953

Batting career:

M	I	NO	Runs	Av
299	524	32	13610	27.66
260	*252*	*17*	*5650*	*24.04*

50	100	CT/ST
64	18	210/1
32	3	69/1

Bowling career:

O	M	R	W	Av
26.1	3	148	0	–

5wI	10wM
–	–

Career best performances:
230 v Worcestershire, Worcester, 1977
130 v Somerset, Bath, 1983*

John Hopkins was born just a six hit away from Maesteg Celtic's cricket ground, so it was no surprise that he and his brother Jeff had careers as professional cricketers. After a short spell on the MCC groundstaff, John made his Glamorgan debut in 1970 as a solid batsman and also an occasional wicketkeeper. Indeed, he created several records by becoming the youngest ever 'keeper in both the Sunday League competition and for Glamorgan in any form of cricket when he kept wicket against Northamptonshire at Sophia Gardens aged 17 years and 68 days.

The regular presence of Eifion Jones behind the stumps allowed John to develop his batting skills during the 1970s and from 1977 he formed a reliable opening partnership with Alan Jones.

In his first season as an opener he compiled a career best 230 against Worcestershire at New Road. At the time, it was the highest post-war Championship score for the Welsh county and it was achieved after he had shared an opening partnership of 253 with Alan Jones.

Hopkins's fluent strokeplay and ability to build long innings drew attention from the England selectors and in 1977/78 he won a Whitbread scholarship to Australia. At the start of 1978 he was selected to play for the MCC against the Pakistani tourists, but this was the closest he came to higher honours.

He duly became the sheet anchor of many Glamorgan innings, both in the County Championship and in one-day competition. Indeed, in 1983 he established another club record with an innings of 130* in the Sunday League fixture against Somerset at Bath. For fourteen years this remained the highest score in the competition by a Glamorgan batsman.

Hopkins was a courageous and determined batsman against the new ball and was particularly brave against the many overseas fast bowlers on the county circuit. He loved to bat and as one colleague fondly remembered, 'the one memory that will always remain in my mind is the sad sight of John Hopkins slowly walking back to the pavilion after being dismissed. Whether he had scored 1 or 101, you felt that his world had come to an end – and to John, it just had!'

Steve James

RHB, 1985-present

Born: Lydney, 7 September 1967

Batting career:

M	I	NO	Runs	Av
172	300	24	11124	40.30
164	*160*	*16*	*5178*	*35.96*

50	100	CT/ST
39	33	144
34	*7*	*38*

Career best performances:

259* v Nottinghamshire, Colwyn Bay, 1999
135 v Combined Univs, Sophia Gardens, 1992

Steve James has been one of the most consistent opening batsmen in county cricket from the mid-1990s. In 1999 he hit the third highest individual score in Glamorgan's history and played the longest ever innings for the county with 259* in almost twelve hours at the crease against Nottinghamshire at Colwyn Bay.

His prolific run-scoring has not gone unnoticed by the England selectors and in 1998 he won two Test caps, although both times he was called up as a late replacement. His first cap came at Lord's in the Second Test with South Africa in 1998, after Mark Butcher had not recovered from a badly bruised thumb. James began with two handsome fours, but then received a brute of a short ball from Allan Donald that he nudged down the leg-side to wicketkeeper Mark Boucher.

James made a duck in the second innings, but was called up again in August for the one-off Test against Sri Lanka at The Oval. It followed Mike Atherton's withdrawal because of back trouble, and all at a time when Steve's wife was about to go into labour in a Cardiff hospital. After making an assured 36 in the first innings, James returned by train to Cardiff to attend the birth of his daughter, before returning to London for the second day's play.

He made his Glamorgan debut at the end of the 1985 season, although heavy rain meant that he never actually got onto the field. The Lydney-born batsman then read Classics at Swansea University before becoming a postgraduate at Cambridge where he won cricket Blues in 1989 and 1990, as well as coming close to winning one for rugby. His finest innings whilst at Cambridge was 131* for the Combined Universities against the 1990 New Zealanders, as the students defeated the tourists by two wickets. They had been set a target of 263 in 71 overs on a turning Fenner's wicket, but James skilfully guided the students home, winning the match with ten balls remaining as he struck his sixteenth four.

After leaving Cambridge, James won a place as Hugh Morris's opening partner and he

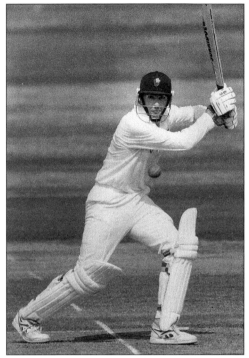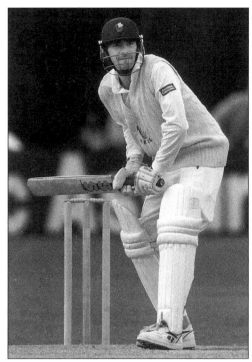

Left: *Steve James square-drives against Middlesex at Sophia Gardens, Cardiff, in 1995.* Right: *Steve James at the crease – a familiar sight for Glamorgan spectators and probably a frustrating one for opposing bowlers.*

developed into a fine opening batsman in both the one-day and four-day forms of the county game. His versatility was confirmed in 1995, when he hit an unbeaten 230 in the Championship match against Leicestershire and finished the season as the country's leading run scorer in the Sunday League with a record 815 runs. His quick running between the wickets and selection of deft strokes have been a feature of the former Monmouth schoolboy's play, as well as his ability to play a long innings. This was evident when he made 235 against Nottinghamshire at Worksop in 1996, with an aggregate of 1,766 runs in first-class cricket over the course of the season.

He continued to be a prolific scorer in 1997, amassing 1,775 runs at an average of 68, and the mild-mannered opener wrote his name into Glamorgan's history books by hitting the winning runs at Taunton as the Welsh side became the County Champions of 1997. During this golden summer, James hit 7 hundreds, including 3 in a row in August, and a vital century in the NatWest Trophy semi-final with Essex. His fine batting was rewarded with Glamorgan's Championship success and the job as vice-captain of the England 'A' team in East Africa and Sri Lanka in 1997/98.

In 1999 James hit his career best double hundred at Colwyn Bay to complete a remarkable sequence of scores against Nottinghamshire. Between 1995 and 1999, the talented Glamorgan opener made scores of 101*, 235, 0, 162, 121 and 259* against the Nottinghamshire bowlers.

James is an excellent fielder and his agile groundwork and safe catching was a feature of Glamorgan's success in the Benson & Hedges competition in 2000. Indeed, it was James who took the final catch in the semi-final victory over Surrey, which saw Glamorgan to the Lord's final.

Javed Miandad

RHB and LB, 1980-1985

Born: Karachi, Pakistan, 12 June 1957

Batting career:

M	I	NO	Runs	Av
83	135	22	6531	57.80
83	*76*	*10*	*3035*	*45.98*

50	100	CT/ST
31	17	50
28	*1*	*21*

Bowling career:

O	M	R	W	Av
254.3	57	851	21	40.52
13.5	*0*	*70*	*2*	*35.00*

5wI	10wM
–	–

Career best performances:
212* v Leicestershire, Swansea, 1984
3/52 v Warwickshire, Edgbaston, 1982
107 v Leicestershire, Leicester, 1981*
1/5 v Essex, Colchester, 1981

Javed Miandad was Pakistan's most valuable batsman during the 1980s and he joined Glamorgan at the start of the decade, having played for Sussex since 1976. During his career with the county, the mercurial strokemaker established a number of batting records, including 8 centuries and 2,083 runs in 1981.

Before leaving the club in 1986, Miandad hit 17 centuries for Glamorgan. Of these, his finest innings in Wales was a majestic double hundred against the 1985 Australians at Neath, during a partnership of 306 for the fourth wicket with fellow Pakistani Younis Ahmed. Away from home, Javed's best innings was an amazing 200 against Essex in 1981, compiled on a crumbling wicket at Colchester and his brilliance nearly resulted in a Glamorgan victory as his team fell just 13 runs short of their unlikely target of 325 on the final day.

Javed had amassed 1,460 runs in 1980, but in 1981 he rewrote the club's record book with 2,083 runs to beat Gilbert Parkhouse's total for the most number of runs in a season. Although this has been subsequently passed by Hugh

Morris and Alan Butcher, Javed's average of 69.43 in 1981 remains as the highest in a season for Glamorgan. During the summer he also struck a record 8 centuries, including 3 in successive innings, with 105 against Warwickshire at Sophia Gardens, followed by 137* and 106 against Somerset at Swansea.

From an early age, Javed had displayed an immense batting talent and a very sharp cricketing brain. He first came to England in 1975 at the age of eighteen, when he played for Pakistan in the inaugural Cricket World Cup. The following year he made his Test debut with a scintillating century against New Zealand at Lahore. Throughout his twenty-year career in the Test arena, his Test batting average never dropped below fifty.

Javed retired from Test cricket in 1993/94 after the series with Zimbabwe as Pakistan's most prolific run scorer with a total of 8,832 Test runs at 52.57. He reappeared in the 1996 World Cup – the sixth time he had played in the competition. He played in 124 Test matches as well as 233 limited-overs internationals.

Viv Jenkins

RHB, RM and occasional WK, 1931-1937

Born: Port Talbot, 2 November 1911

Batting career:

M	I	NO	Runs	Av
44	69	9	1072	17.87

50	100	CT/ST
3	–	10/7

Bowling career:

O	M	R	W	Av
10.1	0	54	2	27.00

5wI	10wM
–	–

Career best performances:
65 v Surrey, The Oval, 1932
1/13 v Surrey, The Oval, 1932

Viv Jenkins was one of the true all-round sporting gentlemen of the 1930s. Besides batting, bowling and keeping wicket for Glamorgan, Jenkins won a double Blue at Oxford, played club rugby for Cardiff, Bridgend, London Welsh, Dover, Kent and the Barbarians, won 14 Welsh rugby caps as full-back between 1932 and 1938, and toured South Africa as the vice-captain of the British Lions party in 1938.

The former Llandovery schoolboy made his county debut for Glamorgan in 1931 whilst an undergraduate at Oxford and after leaving university he went into teaching in Kent. He subsequently played for Glamorgan during his school holidays and his all-round ball skills and athletic fielding must have made captain Maurice Turnbull wish that Jenkins had been available on a more regular basis.

His earliest appearances in 1931 had been as a wicketkeeper after regular 'keeper Trevor Every was injured and, in his second appearance behind the stumps, against Worcestershire at Pontypridd, he pulled off three sharp stumpings as Worcestershire's batsmen struggled against the spin of Clay and Ryan.

Jenkins retained his place in the side when Every regained fitness and in the fixture against Surrey at the Arms Park, Jenkins played a match-winning innings. Glamorgan had been set a target of 215 runs in 165 minutes and, with the scoreboard on 146-6, a Surrey victory looked on the cards. However, Jenkins had other ideas and played a series of forcing strokes in his unbeaten 40 that saw Glamorgan home by three wickets with minutes to spare.

After the Second World War, Jenkins became a leading sports journalist with the *News of the World*, as well as serving as rugby correspondent of *The Sunday Times*. He also edited the *Rothman's Rugby Union Yearbook* for many years and is currently president of Glamorgan's Former Players' Association.

Alan Jones MBE

LHB and OB, 1957-1983

Born: Velindre, 4 November 1938

Batting career:

M	I	NO	Runs	Av
610	1102	71	34056	33.03
283	*280*	*21*	*7061*	*27.26*

50	100	CT/ST
186	52	276
41	*2*	*73*

Bowling Career:

O	M	R	W	Av
58.5	15	249	1	249.00
5.3	*0*	*27*	*3*	*9.00*

5wI	10wM
–	–

Career best performances:
204* v Hampshire, Basingstoke, 1980
1/41 v Worcestershire, Worcester, 1970
124 v Warwickshire, Edgbaston, 1976*
3/21 v Northants, Wellingborough, 1975

Alan Jones holds a strong claim to being Glamorgan's greatest batsman, with over 40,000 runs to his name in all forms of the game for the county. Indeed, no batsman is likely to surpass his record of 34,056 first-class runs and 7,061 in limited-overs games. He also holds the record for having passed over 1,000 runs on 23 consecutive occasions and scoring a club record of 52 first-class centuries. Given his outstanding achievements, it makes it even more remarkable that he never won any Test caps for England.

The stylish left-handed batsman joined the county staff in 1955 and in 1957 he made his county debut in Glamorgan's middle order. In the early 1960s he moved up to open the batting and began his prolific career as an opener. By the time he retired in 1983, he had opened with a host of other fine players, including Bernard Hedges, Gilbert Parkhouse, Roy Fredericks, Roger Davis and John Hopkins.

In 1962 Alan recorded his maiden century against Sussex at Hastings and in the following year hit hundreds in both innings against Somerset at Glastonbury, being on the field of play for the whole match. Other highlights in first-class cricket included 161* against the West Indies at Swansea in 1966, 99 against Australia in the famous victory at Swansea in 1968 and a career best 204* against Hampshire at Basingstoke in 1980 at the age of forty-one. He also shared in a record opening partnership of 330 with Roy Fredericks against Northamptonshire at Swansea in 1972.

Jones also scored heavily in limited-overs games. In 1978 he hit Glamorgan's first ever Sunday League century with 110* against Gloucestershire at Sophia Gardens. He led Glamorgan against Middlesex in the Gillette Cup final in 1977 and this was the highlight of his county leadership between 1976 and 1978.

Alan combined a solid technique with admirable powers of concentration. With his prolific and consistent record, it is surprising that he was constantly overlooked by the England selectors. In 1970 Alan was chosen to appear in the series with the Rest of the World, which at the time was considered to be worthy of Test status. He was given a cap and blazer, but the

Alan Jones straight drives Michael Holding against the West Indians at Swansea in 1976.

Alan Jones pulls against Lancashire in 1976.

bureaucrats at Lord's later stripped the series of Test status, depriving the loyal Glamorgan opener of the highest honour. Whilst never having officially played for England, Jones can at least claim to have appeared for an Australian XI in first-class cricket. This unlikely honour came his way in 1963/64, when Alan was playing for Western Australia and was drafted into a combined XI for the match against the South Africans at Perth. Whilst in Australia, Jones recorded half-centuries against Queensland and South Australia. He tasted more success on foreign fields during the MCC tour to Ceylon and the Far East in 1969/70. After hitting 112 against Ceylon at Colombo, Jones hit 102* in Bangkok and 104* against Hong Kong.

In 1982 he received the MBE in the Queen's Honours List in recognition of his devoted efforts for the Welsh county. He played his final Championship match against Hampshire at Southampton at the end of the 1983 season, and took over as club coach. He remained as director of coaching until retiring in 1998 after a lifetime of loyal and wholehearted service to Glamorgan.

Alan Lewis Jones
LHB, 1973-1986

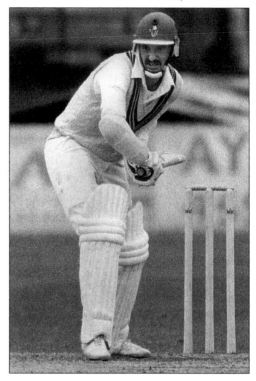

Born: Alltwen, 1 June 1957

Batting career:

M	I	NO	Runs	Av
160	278	24	6548	25.78
111	*104*	*4*	*2047*	*20.47*

50	100	CT/ST
36	5	104
9	*–*	*35*

Bowling career:

O	M	R	W	Av
15.5	0	152	1	152.00
0.4	*0*	*5*	*0*	*–*

5wI	10wM
–	–

Career best performances:
132 v Hampshire, Sophia Gardens, 1984
1/60 v Yorkshire, Sophia Gardens, 1984
82 v Warwickshire, Edgbaston, 1982

Alan Lewis Jones emerged during the mid-1970s as a bold and attractive opening batsman. He became one of the club's youngest ever players when he made his first-class debut as a sixteen year old against Gloucestershire in 1973 at Bristol and he subsequently played for Young England. In 1975 the eighteen-year-old Lewis Jones showed his immense promise against the touring Australians at Swansea, hitting a rapid 55 during a century partnership for the first wicket, and repeatedly hooked and pulled the experienced Aussie pacemen to the boundary.

The young left-hander was groomed as the long-term successor to Alan Jones and, after completing his college studies, A.L. secured a regular place in the county's side. It was surprising that for someone with such a wide array of strikes that it took him until 1984 to register his maiden Championship hundred. He reached this landmark against Gloucestershire at Sophia Gardens and it proved to be such a huge boost to his confidence that he went on to record four further centuries that season, including a career best 132 against Hampshire, 122 against Middlesex at Swansea, 114 against Essex at Southend and 100 against Somerset at Taunton.

A.L. ended the 1984 season with a career best 1,811 runs in first-class cricket, and he seemed poised to confirm his potential. However, in 1985 he injured his shoulder whilst diving to stop the ball in the opening Sunday League match with Kent at Sophia Gardens, and spent several months on the sidelines. It sadly proved to be a serious injury, as afterwards A.L. found difficulty fielding and throwing the ball. After a further operation and a period of rehabilitation, he was forced to retire in 1986. He led the Glamorgan Colts in 1987 in their matches in the South Wales Cricket Association, before concentrating on his career with a building society and taking up a position in Maidenhead.

Closs Jones
RHB and OB, 1934-1946

Born: Briton Ferry, 14 December 1911
Died: Briton Ferry, 14 April 1989

Batting career:

M	I	NO	Runs	Av
100	142	30	2016	18.00

50	100	CT/ST
7	2	42

Bowling career:

O	M	R	W	Av
1036.1	165	3299	102	32.14

5wI	10wM
6	1

Career best performances:
132 v Cambridge University, Swansea, 1938
7/79 v Sussex, Cardiff Arms Park, 1937

Had his career not been interrupted twice, Closs Jones would surely have won Test honours with England. The off-spinner initially played as an amateur in 1934, before turning professional in 1937. During that season he began with five-wicket hauls against Kent and Lancashire, followed by 7/79 against Sussex, before taking a match haul of 10/94 against the New Zealanders at Cardiff as Glamorgan defeated the tourists by 6 wickets.

This resulted in his selection for the Rest of the World side which played the MCC in their 150th Anniversary match, and the England selectors had a chance to assess the credentials of the twenty-five-year-old Welshman. However, soon afterwards, he badly injured his shoulder and lost form, taking just 14 wickets in the last two months of the season.

Jones regained his form in the Glamorgan side in 1938 and sought to re-establish himself as one of the country's best young off-spinners. He also worked hard on his batting skills, striking a career best 132 against Cambridge University at Swansea, as well as 105* against Kent at Tonbridge in 1939. But just when he seemed back to his best, his career was halted again by the outbreak of the Second World War. Jones appeared in several of the county's fund-raising friendlies during 1944 and 1945, but the war blighted his attempts to rediscover his form as a spin bowler. By the time the County Championship restarted in 1946, Jones had opted for a career away from professional cricket. Even so, he agreed to help the county out in 1946, but he retired midway through the summer to work at the Briton Ferry Steel Company.

Jones continued to play for many years in club cricket in the South Wales Cricket Association and helped many promising young players in the Neath area. Even when well into his seventies, Jones would pass on tips to the youngsters and Steve Barwick was amongst those to have benefited from Jones's coaching.

Eifion Jones

RHB and WK, 1961-1983

Born: Velindre, 25 June 1942

Batting career:

M	I	NO	Runs	Av
405	591	119	8341	17.67
292	*226*	*65*	*2236*	*13.89*

50	100	CT/ST
26	3	840/93
1	*–*	*253/43*

Bowling career:

O	M	R	W	Av
0.3	0	5	0	–
2.0	*1*	*10*	*0*	*–*

5wI	10wM
–	–

Career best performances:
146* v Sussex, Hove, 1968
67 v Hertfordshire, Swansea, 1969*

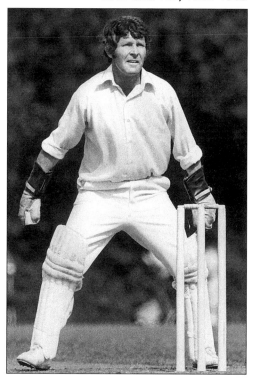

Many Glamorgan supporters believe that Eifion Jones was the best of the top-class group of wicketkeepers to have succeeded Haydn Davies as Glamorgan's man behind the stumps. Jones had joined the Glamorgan staff at the start of the 1960s as a specialist right-handed batsman, but, as Wilf Wooller remembered, 'there was something about his stocky stature and quick alert movements that suggested to the coach Phil Clift that Jones might make a top-class wicketkeeper. And so it proved.' With coaching from Phil Clift, Eifion developed his skills as a 'keeper and was the club's regular gloveman from 1968 until 1982. He retired at the end of the 1983 season with a club record of 933 dismissals to his name in first-class cricket.

Eifion rarely dropped a chance standing up or back and his almost faultless displays for the Welsh county almost won him a place on England's Ashes tour in 1970/71. During the previous summer, the stocky wicketkeeper had claimed more victims than anyone else in the country. He also took 74 dismissals in 1969 as Glamorgan won the County Championship for the second time in their history but, like his older brother Alan, Eifion narrowly missed out on selection for the winter tour.

In 1970 he established new club records by taking 94 victims in first-class cricket and making 7 dismissals in an innings against Cambridge University at Cambridge. In 1968 he had also created a record for the highest score by a wicketkeeper, making 146* against Sussex at Hove, and sharing a partnership of 230 with his brother for the third wicket.

Eifion also holds the record for the most number of appearances for Glamorgan in the Sunday League, playing on 212 occasions. During this time, he claimed a further 223 dismissals to take his overall tally in every form of cricket to over 1,000 – a worthy reward for his years of loyal service to the Welsh club.

Jeff Jones
RHB and LF, 1960-1968

Born: Dafen, 10 December 1941

Batting career:

M	I	NO	Runs	Av
157	180	69	395	3.55
9	*6*	*3*	*20*	*6.67*

50	100	CT/ST
–	–	36
–	–	*2*

Bowling Career:

O	M	R	W	Av
3904.4	979	9583	408	23.48
112.3	*25*	*319*	*22*	*14.50*

5wI	10wM
16	–

Career best performances:
20 v Sussex, Arms Park, 1965
8/11 v Leicestershire, Leicester, 1965
7 v Essex, Neath, 1966
4/12 v Northamptonshire, 1966

Jeff Jones was one of the fastest ever bowlers to play for Glamorgan and he was certainly the quickest left-armer in the club's history. During the 1960s, he spearheaded the Glamorgan attack and went on to win 15 Test caps for England. This still stands today as the most number of appearances by a Glamorgan cricketer in Tests for England and had it not been for a serious elbow injury, Jones would surely have won over twice this number of caps.

Jones's bowling for Llanelli CC at the end of the 1950s drew the attention of the Glamorgan talent scouts and he joined the county in 1960. He made his first-class debut later in the season against Kent at Blackheath and by 1962 he was the regular new ball bowler, extracting pace and bounce from a fast, high action. In 1962 he took a hat-trick against Yorkshire at Harrogate and his outstanding potential was recognised by the England selectors, who chose him for the MCC tour to East Africa and India. It was during the Indian leg of the tour that he ironically won his England cap before his Glamorgan one, as he made his Test debut at Bombay in 1963/64.

An injury restricted his appearances in 1964, but he was back to full fitness in 1965 and produced career best figures of 13-9-11-8 on a damp green wicket at Grace Road as Leicestershire were bowled out for 40. Jones finished the season with 84 wickets and won his county cap. He returned to the England fold on their 1965/66 tour to Australia and New Zealand, where he found the hard and quick wickets to his liking. After a match return of 7/98 against Western Australia at Perth, he came into the side for the Second Test and held his place for the rest of the series. Indeed, during the Fourth Test at Adelaide he took 6/118 to record the best analysis by a Glamorgan bowler in international cricket.

He returned home in the spring of 1966 as the leading wicket-taker, with 56 scalps to his name in all the games on tour, and he played in the first two Tests of the series at home to the West Indies in 1966. The following season, Jones took 100 wickets in all first-class matches and was chosen to tour the West Indies in 1967/68 with the MCC. The Second Test at Kingston

Jeff Jones keeps Nottinghamshire batsman Mike Harris firmly on the back foot at Swansea in 1967, watched by Peter Walker and wicketkeeper David Evans.

will be chiefly remembered for the infamous riot, but it should not be forgotten that Jones took 5/129 from 44 hostile overs. It was a successful series for England and it was Jones's modest abilities as a number eleven batsman that ultimately helped England to win as he blocked out the last over of the final Test from Lance Gibbs at Georgetown, Guyana.

Jones was poised to establish himself in the England squad for many years and it seemed he would play a key role in the 1968 Ashes series but, sadly, he damaged shoulder and elbow ligaments at Ilford early in the summer and missed the rest of the season. Worse followed as a specialist diagnosed arthritis in his elbow joint and a severe wearing of the bone. Jeff tried to modify his action and return to county cricket, but it was to no avail and he was forced into premature retirement from first-class cricket.

In recent years he has played in club cricket as a spinner, as well as appearing for the Old England side. His son, Simon, followed in his father's footsteps by joining the Glamorgan staff on leaving school and made his debut in 1998.

Jeff Jones, Glamorgan's fastest ever left-arm bowler.

Willie Jones
LHB and SLA, 1937-1958

Born: Carmarthen, 31 October 1916
Died: Gloucester, 25 July 1996

Batting career:

M	I	NO	Runs	Av
340	555	63	13270	27.00

50	100	CT/ST
76	11	117

Bowling career:

O	M	R	W	Av
1926.2	438	5620	189	29.73

5wI	10wM
3	–

Career best performances:
212* v Essex, Brentwood, 1948
5/50 v Kent, Gravesend, 1949

The mild-mannered Willie Jones created what so far has been a unique feat in Glamorgan's history when he hit two double hundreds within the space of a fortnight. This achievement came in 1948 with 207 against Kent at Gravesend, followed by an unbeaten 212 against Essex at Brentwood during a record-breaking partnership of 313 for the third wicket with Emrys Davies.

The left-handed batsman and spin bowler joined the Glamorgan staff in 1935 and initially learnt his trade with the county's Second XI, playing in the Minor County Championship. In 1937 Maurice Turnbull decided to improve the county's fielding by drafting the twenty-year-old Jones into the first team and, as befitting a talented rugby player, he soon impressed with his swift running and safe catching, whether close to the wicket or in the outfield.

His fielding and developing batting skills won him a regular place in the Glamorgan team from 1938 and, in the years either side of the Second World War, Jones mixed playing

county cricket in the summer with club rugby during the winter for Llanelli, Neath and Gloucester. With other rugby players in the Glamorgan side, there was always a lot of friendly banter and leg pulling in the county's dressing room about who was the finest player. Indeed, Willie would wager with Wilf Wooller that he could kick a rugby ball further than the Glamorgan skipper: often after play at the Arms Park, the pair would have a kicking contest on the adjoining rugby field.

Willie Jones became the mainstay of Glamorgan's middle order after the Second World War and he became a gifted strokemaker, always ready to punish any wayward deliveries. On seven occasions, Jones passed 1,000 runs for the season, and demonstrated a sound and steady technique, especially against spin bowling. Amongst his finest strokes were a rasping square-cut and flashing off-drive, and Gloucestershire's prolific spinner Tom Goddard claimed that Willie was one of the few batsmen he could never bowl a length to.

Willie Jones batting against South Africa's Percy Mansell at Swansea in 1951.

In 1948 Willie scored 1,656 runs in first-class matches and was chosen to appear in the 1949 Test trial. However, he sustained an injury while fielding and missed much of the season, just when staking a claim to a place in the England side. He regained fitness in 1950, but no further opportunities came his way to impress at the highest level. Despite this, he remained a prolific run-maker in the county game until retiring in 1958 and frequently his aggressive batting belied his quiet, shy and reserved manner. As John Arlott once wrote: 'Willie Jones had a face you remember for its immense range of expression – eyes sparkling at some new story, tensely anxious when the game is in a crucial state, utterly wretched at having done less than he hoped in some important innings, but most memorable of all, standing, his hair sticking flat to his forehead, after an innings that had put Glamorgan right, shyness struggling with sheer delight – Willie in a state of bubbling, but silent happiness.'

Willie Jones.

Peter Judge
RHB and RFM, 1939-1947

Born: Cricklewood, 23 May 1916
Died: London, 4 March 1992

Batting career:

M	I	NO	Runs	Av
54	67	24	332	7.12

50	100	CT/ST
–	–	29

Bowling career:

O	M	R	W	Av
1175.3	221	3475	138	25.18

5wI	10wM
3	–

Career best performances:
40 v Worcestershire, Ebbw Vale, 1946
8/75 v Yorkshire, Bradford, 1939

Peter Judge has a unique claim to fame – he was dismissed by two consecutive balls within a minute during Glamorgan's match with the Indians in 1946. This unusual distinction took place at the Arms Park when, after Judge had been bowled by the last ball of Glamorgan's first innings, captain Johnnie Clay decided to reverse the batting order so as to inject life into the fixture which was heading for a tame draw and provide some entertainment for the sizeable crowd. Clay and Judge stayed out in the middle as the Indian captain reset the field, but barely a minute after being bowled, Judge was on his way back to the Cardiff pavilion after being bowled again by the first ball of the second innings!

Judge began his career with Middlesex after a promising schoolboy career at St Paul's School in London. He also played for The Rest against the MCC Schools at Lord's before playing for Middlesex 8 times between 1933 and 1934. He then joined Buckinghamshire and subsequently played League cricket in Yorkshire and Cumbria, before joining Glamorgan in 1939. The well-travelled right-arm seamer took 69 wickets in his first full season, including career best figures of 8/75 against Yorkshire at Bradford.

During the Second World War, he served with the RAF in the London area and secured enough leave to play for both the British Empire XI and a Lord's XI in the friendly matches which helped to raise money for the war effort. He was subsequently posted to Gloucester and then India, where he added to his list of teams by appearing for Bengal and the Europeans.

He returned to Glamorgan in 1946 and bowled well once again. Among his haul of 64 wickets was a spell of 10.1-1-23-7 against Derbyshire at Cardiff Arms Park, as Judge fully exploited a damp wicket and blustery crosswind as Derbyshire were all out for a paltry 40. He was then struck down with a foot injury in 1947 and only appeared in three games before bouts of ill-health led to him giving up professional cricket.

His overall first-class record was 173 wickets at 27, but this would have been much better had the war not intervened. As a result, Judge will be most remembered for that rather unique distinction with the bat against the 1946 Indians.

Jacques Kallis
RHB and RFM, 1999-present

Born: South Africa, 16 October 1975

Batting career:

M	I	NO	Runs	Av
6	9	0	362	40.22
8	*8*	*2*	*496*	*82.67*

50	100	CT/ST
2	1	3
2	*2*	*2*

Bowling career:

O	M	R	W	Av
95.0	12	345	11	31.36
39.3	*3*	*151*	*6*	*25.16*

5wI	10wM
–	–

Career best performances:
101 v Nottinghamshire, Colwyn Bay, 1999
3/52 v Somerset, Taunton, 1999
155 v Surrey, Pontypridd, 1999*
2/27 v Durham, Chester-le-Street, 1999

Jacques Kallis, the gifted South African all-rounder, joined Glamorgan during 1999 after playing for the Springboks in the World Cup. A groin injury delayed his debut until the National League game on 25 July against Surrey at Pontypridd, but it turned out to be a debut worth waiting for as Kallis produced an explosive display of clean hitting, to score 155* – the highest ever individual innings in the competition for the Welsh county and the best performance ever on debut for the club.

Kallis added a further one day hundred later in the season against Somerset, as well as a Championship century against Nottinghamshire at Colwyn Bay, during which time he shared a partnership of 216 with Steve James for the second wicket. His commitments with South Africa will prevent him from playing for Glamorgan in 2000, but he has agreed to return in 2001 and Glamorgan's spectators will be looking forward to more classical strokeplay and hostile fast-medium bowling from the gifted South African.

Kallis showed rich promise at high school and he made his debut for Western Province as an eighteen year old in 1993/94. After hours of coaching from Duncan Fletcher, the Western Province (and later Glamorgan and England) coach, Kallis progressed into the South African team during the 1995/96 series with England.

After adjusting to the demands of international cricket, Kallis has developed into one of the finest all-rounders currently playing Test cricket and, by the start of the 2000 season, Kallis had already played in 34 Tests and 80 one-day internationals. All Glamorgan supporters will be hoping that Kallis can return to the Welsh county in 2001 and continue his great deeds with both bat and ball.

George Lavis
RHB and RM, 1928-1949

Born: Sebastopol, 17 August 1908
Died: Pontypool, 29 July 1956

Batting career:

M	I	NO	Runs	Av
206	312	43	4957	18.42

50	100	CT/ST
23	3	71

Bowling career:

O	M	R	W	Av
2741.0	515	7768	156	49.79

5wI	10wM
–	–

Career best performances:
154 v Worcestershire, Arms Park, 1934
4/55 v Sussex, Arms Park, 1933

The career figures of George Lavis never did justice to this more than useful all-rounder. But, after the Second World War, he gained recognition as an energetic and popular coach to the Glamorgan side, duly becoming one of the best in a long line of highly respected coaches to have groomed the county's young players. From 1946 until his sudden death in 1956, Lavis acted as Glamorgan's coach and a host of young cricketers owe their later success for Glamorgan, as well as England, to Lavis's wise words and the long hours of patient guidance in the club's nets.

The Monmouthshire-born batsman made his first-class debut back in 1928 as a right-handed batsman and seam bowler. He secured a regular place in the middle order during the early 1930s and proceeded to hit three centuries, including a career best 154 against Worcestershire in 1934, while sharing a fourth-wicket partnership of 236 with Cyril Smart. Lavis's most successful season as a player was in 1934, when he scored 883 runs in first-class games and claimed 26 wickets with his brisk medium-pace bowling. However, he had rather modest seasons with bat and ball in

1936 and again in 1937, before leaving the county's playing staff and moving to Dundee, where he played for Forfarshire.

After serving with the RAF, Lavis returned to South Wales after the Second World War, and was appointed Glamorgan's coach as they rebuilt after the war and the loss, amongst others, of their influential leader, Maurice Turnbull. Lavis also agreed to play for the county again, whenever Glamorgan were short of players, and he duly appeared on an infrequent basis until 1949. He took a testimonial in 1950, before concentrating full-time on his coaching duties and carefully producing the next generation of Glamorgan cricketers.

Lavis also had a fine tenor voice which was often heard echoing around dressing rooms up and down the country as the team wound down after a busy day's play. Lavis was Glamorgan's twelfth man at Bournemouth in 1948 when the team won the County Championship and it was not long after winning the title that his voice rang out around the pavilion as he and the Welsh team cheerfully celebrated their success.

Roland Lefebvre

RHB and RM, 1993-1995

Born: Rotterdam, 7 February 1963

Batting career:

M	I	NO	Runs	Av
34	45	6	779	19.97
59	*34*	*15*	*337*	*17.74*

50	100	CT/ST
1	–	16
–	–	*38*

Bowling career:

O	M	R	W	Av
1070.0	313	2454	75	32.72
508.2	*75*	*1636*	*83*	*19.71*

5wI	10wM
1	–

Career best performances:
50 v Worcestershire, Worcester, 1993
6/45 v Oxford University, The Parks, 1995
36 v Northamptonshire, Pentyrch, 1993*
4/23 v Durham, Hartlepool, 1994

The signing of Roland Lefebvre during the winter of 1992/93 from Somerset proved to be a masterstroke as Glamorgan acquired the services of a most effective opening bowler in one-day cricket. Week after week, the Dutch seamer bowled with exemplary control and a full and nagging length to frustrate and contain opposing batsmen. Few opponents managed to get on top of him and his accuracy with the ball was a key ingredient behind Glamorgan winning the Sunday League in 1993.

Lefebvre's greatest asset was probably his skill at bowling 'death balls' at the end of a one-day game. He cheerfully spent many hours practising these full-length deliveries and could be relied upon to bowl six successive balls in roughly the same spot, restricting the batsman often to no more than a hastily scrambled single or leg bye, when the asking rate required something more substantial.

Amongst his finest spells for Glamorgan were 4/23 in the Sunday League game against Durham in 1994 and a return of 11-5-13-2 in the NatWest Trophy quarter-final against Worcestershire at Swansea in 1993. In this latter match, Roland conceded just two runs from his opening six overs and bowled Tim Curtis, before returning to bowl a fine sequence of 'death balls', giving away just 11 runs in his final 6 overs.

Lefebvre was also a capable lower-order batsman, hitting a first-class hundred for Somerset against Worcestershire in 1991. He also pulled off some remarkable catches whilst with Glamorgan and his athletic efforts in the field, together with his accuracy with the ball, made him a firm favourite with Glamorgan's supporters.

Before joining Glamorgan, Lefebvre played for Somerset between 1990 and 1992, and took 7/15 in their NatWest Trophy match against Devon in 1990. He also played for Canterbury in 1990/91 and claimed career best bowling figures of 6/53 against Auckland. A severe groin injury forced him to retire from professional cricket at the end of 1995, but he has still managed to play in club cricket in South Africa and Holland, who he has represented in the ICC Trophy since 1986.

Tony Lewis
RHB and LB, 1955-1974

Born: Uplands, Swansea, 6 July 1938

Batting career:

M	I	NO	Runs	Av
315	546	52	15003	30.37
93	*90*	*4*	*2061*	*23.97*

50	100	CT/ST
81	21	155
12	*–*	*27*

Bowling career:

O	M	R	W	Av
55.1	3	306	4	76.50
2.2	*0*	*16*	*0*	*–*

5wI	10wM
–	–

Career best performances:
223 v Kent, Gravesend, 1966
3/18 v Somerset, Neath, 1967
96 v Hertfordshire, Swansea, 1969

In December 1972, Tony Lewis became the first Glamorgan player to lead England in a Test match and joined an elite group of players to lead his side to victory in what was his debut at international level. Lewis's elevation to Test cricket came at the age of thirty-four and it was a worthy reward for his consistent run-scoring and the way he had proudly and astutely led the Welsh county to the Championship title in 1969.

Lewis was brought up in Neath, with the family home close to the town's cricket and rugby ground at The Gnoll. The youngster took every opportunity to watch the winter and summer sporting action, and at Neath Grammar School he developed into a talented cricketer and rugby player. He won representative honours with the Welsh Schools and was invited to the Glamorgan nets in Cardiff. But he, quite literally, had other strings to his bow, as the schoolboy showed rich promise as a violinist and was preparing to go on the Welsh National Youth Orchestra's summer tour in 1955,

when he received a call up to make his Championship debut for Glamorgan against Leicestershire at Cardiff. This was, however, not a fairytale debut, as Lewis was dismissed for a duck by the wily Australian spinner Jack Walsh.

Despite his initial failure, the Glamorgan selectors showed great faith in the young amateur and with the help of Wilf Wooller, the Glamorgan captain, Lewis went to Christ's College, Cambridge, to read History. Lewis duly became a double Blue and after playing club rugby for Neath, Pontypool and Gloucester, a knee injury forced Lewis to concentrate on his cricket career.

During the early 1960s, Lewis mixed playing for Cambridge in the first part of the season, with Championship cricket for Glamorgan during his summer vacations. In 1962 he was appointed captain of the Light Blues and fittingly rounded off his successful sporting career for the university with 103* in the Varsity Match. He continued his good form after leaving and shared in a record partnership of 238 with Alan Jones for the second wicket against Sussex at Hastings.

Lewis subsequently became a regular in the county's middle order and he developed into a dashing stroke-player, with a wide range of elegant drives and deft cuts. His most successful summer was in 1966 when he became the second batsman in the club's history to pass 2,000 runs. During the season, he compiled 2,052 runs, with 5 centuries, and hit a career best 223 against Kent at Gravesend.

For many years, Lewis had been groomed by Wilf Wooller as a future captain and in 1967 he took over the leadership, moulding a successful playing unit. He developed into a sound tactician and, under his shrewd leadership, Glamorgan rose to third place in 1968, before winning the Championship outright in 1969, with the side remaining unbeaten throughout the summer.

Lewis proved most adept at getting the best out of the players at his disposal and he was widely regarded on the county circuit as the finest captain yet to play Test cricket. Following Glamorgan's Championship success, he was rewarded with the captaincy of the MCC party to Ceylon and the Far East in 1969/70. This also confirmed his standing in English cricket, so when in 1972 Test skipper Ray Illingworth and experienced batsman Mike Smith both announced they would not be going on the winter tour, the England selectors had little hesitation in inviting Lewis to lead the side to India, Pakistan and Sri Lanka.

On 5 December 1972, Lewis led out the England side in the opening match of the tour at Hyderabad against a President's XI. Barely a fortnight later, he led the team out at the Feroz Shah Kotla ground in New Delhi in the First Test of the series with India. Like his own county debut in 1955 for Glamorgan, Lewis's first innings at Test level ended in a duck. However, he made an unbeaten 70 in the second innings and shared a partnership of 101 with Tony Greig to guide the side to victory shortly after lunch on Christmas Day – their first win in India since 1951/52.

In the Fourth Test at Kanpur, Lewis arrived at the crease with England's score on 48-2, before counter-attacking the canny Indian spinners, mixing watchful defence with positive strokeplay. He frequently went down the pitch to loft the spinners high over mid-off and mid-on, and went on to record his maiden Test hundred with a most praiseworthy 125.

Lewis's efforts in the sub-continent, both as a batsman and a captain, drew favourable comments from the Press and several writers felt that he had proved himself to be the heir apparent to Ray Illingworth, who was over forty and nearing the end of his Test career. For the opening Test of the 1973 series with New Zealand, Illingworth was nominated captain, with Lewis playing as a specialist batsman, and observers suggested that this was part of a gradual handover phase, with Lewis likely to take the side to the West Indies during the winter.

However, Lewis aggravated his old knee injury and withdrew from the Second Test. After missing several weeks of cricket, he returned to a Glamorgan side who by now were in a rebuilding period, following the retirement of several senior players. Overall, morale was low within the club and at the end of 1973 Lewis was surprised at being only offered a match contract. So whilst the England side visited the Caribbean, Lewis contemplated his future. He loyally played in the early games of the 1974 season, but with his knee continuing to give him problems, he announced his retirement from the county game in July.

He has subsequently become a highly regarded cricket writer, besides being a member of the *Test Match Special* commentary team and the anchorman for BBC television's coverage of Test and domestic cricket as well as chairman of the Welsh Tourist Board. Lewis has remained closely involved with Glamorgan, acting as the club's chairman and, latterly, as president. In 1998 he was also elected president of the MCC and it was fitting that his term of office should be in the year when Lord's and the county grounds of England and Wales played host to the Cricket World Cup.

Euros Lewis
LHB and OB, 1961-1966

Born: Llanelli, 31 January 1942

Batting career:

M	I	NO	Runs	Av
95	150	10	2169	15.49
6	*5*	*0*	*117*	*23.40*

50	100	CT/ST
11	–	53
1	–	*1*

Bowling career:

O	M	R	W	Av
1297.3	363	3821	151	25.30

5wI	10wM
7	–

Career best performances:
80 v Sussex, Arms Park, 1965
8/89 v Kent, Swansea, 1965
78 v Worcestershire, Neath, 1963

Euros Lewis had a short, and at times quite successful, career with Glamorgan during the 1960s. The left-handed batsman and off-spin bowler made his Championship debut in August 1961 against Somerset at Weston-Super-Mare, making 23 and 40, followed by an assured 58 against Gloucestershire at Cheltenham. His bold, free hitting as an opening batsman secured Lewis a place in the side for the rest of the season and he continued to impress with 70 against Warwickshire at Edgbaston.

Lewis also worked hard at his spin bowling and was able to supplement the first choice spin of Don Shepherd and Jim Pressdee. Now that he had two strings to his bow, Lewis dropped down the order in 1963, but he remained an aggressive strokemaker batting at number six or seven. In 1965 he had a memorable match against Sussex at the Arms Park. He initially hit a dashing 80, before returning the remarkable figures of 2.2-1-1-4, polishing off the Sussex second innings in the space of just fourteen balls.

Some of the highlights of Lewis's career with Glamorgan came at St Helen's, as the Welsh spinner fully exploited the dry and dusty Swansea wickets. It was there in 1964 that Lewis was a member of the Glamorgan side that defeated the Australians by 36 runs and at the same ground the following year Lewis returned career best bowling figures of 8/89 in the six-wicket victory over Kent and won his county cap.

However, he proved to be inconsistent and Lewis's relationship with the Welsh club became strained. At the end of the 1966 season, he left Glamorgan to join Sussex, who no doubt had been impressed by the havoc he had caused with both bat and ball at Cardiff the previous year. He duly won his Sussex cap in 1967 after making 553 runs in the Championship, besides taking 59 wickets. But once again his form proved to be erratic, with 320 runs in 1968 plus 40 wickets and a mere 317 runs in the Championship in 1969 at an average of 9.90. He met with modest success with the ball, picking up 42 wickets at 30 runs apiece, and was released by the English county at the end of the 1969 season.

Mike Llewellyn
LHB and OB, 1970-1982

Born: Clydach, 27 November 1953

Batting career:

M	I	NO	Runs	Av
136	215	30	4288	23.71
139	*133*	*25*	*2473*	*22.90*

50	100	CT/ST
20	3	87
10	*–*	*41*

Bowling career:

O	M	R	W	Av
227.1	62	615	23	26.73

5wI	10wM
–	–

Career best performances:
129* v Oxford University, Oxford, 1977
4/35 v Oxford Uniersity, Oxford, 1970
79 v Gloucestershire, Bristol, 1977*

Mike Llewellyn nearly became one of the few players in cricket history to strike a ball over the tall and imposing pavilion at Lord's. His feat came during the 1977 Gillette Cup final against Middlesex and the aggressive left-hander began his innings with two fours and a six off Mike Gatting. Then came his enormous blow, off the bowling of England off-spinner John Emburey, as Llewellyn hit the ball into a gutter on the roof of the famous building.

This was quite literally the high point in Llewellyn's thirteen-year career with Glamorgan. He had played initially, aged 16 years and 202 days, as a batsman and off-spinner against Oxford University at Oxford in 1970, and in 1972 he became the club's youngest centurion with an innings of 112* against Cambridge University at Swansea, aged just 18 years and 213 days.

He failed to live up to his youthful promise and, despite playing some forceful innings during the mid-1970s, found life harder in Championship cricket, especially up against a diet of fast bowling. Indeed, Llewellyn only struck one Championship century during his career, making 106* against Worcestershire at Swansea in 1979, and he never managed to pass 1,000 runs in a season for the club. In 1977 he amassed 842 first-class runs, followed by 849 in 1978, with seven half-centuries.

His maiden Championship century in 1979 suggested that he had turned the corner, but the left-hander's form rather fell away during 1979 and 1980, both in Championship and limited overs cricket. He duly left the staff at the end of the 1982 season and went on to play Minor County cricket for Wiltshire.

Willie Llewelyn
RHB and RM, 1889-1893

Born: Ynysgerwn, 1 April 1868
Died: Penllegaer, 24 August 1893

Batting career:

M	I	NO	Runs	Av
(14	25	0	418	16.72)

50	100	CT/ST
(3	–	10)

Bowling career:

O	M	R	W	Av
(58.5	11	174	6	29.00)

5wI	10wM
(1	–)

Career best performances:
(99 v Monmouthshire, Arms Park, 1893)
(5 wickets v Devon, Swansea, 1893)

Willie Llewelyn might have been one of the greatest batsmen in Glamorgan's Minor County days but, just when on the verge of an illustrious career, he took his life in August 1893 by shooting himself in the grounds of Penllegaer House, just a few weeks before his marriage to the daughter of Lord Dynevor.

Llewelyn was the son of Sir J.T.D. Llewelyn, the squire of Penllegaer, who was rightly called 'The Father of Glamorgan cricket' as he was the man who had convened the meeting in July 1888 at which the county club was founded. Willie Llewelyn had been educated at Eton College, where he won a place in the school's eleven, and also won the Public Schools Racquets competition in both 1886 and 1887.

In 1888 Willie went to Oxford and in 1889 was chosen in the Glamorgan side which recorded their first ever victory by defeating Surrey Club and Ground at The Oval by six wickets. In 1890, and again in 1891, he won a Blue at Oxford, besides striking a career best 116 in 1890 against A.J. Webbe's XI. The undergraduate also captained the Glamorgan side on occasions and was invited to appear in many of the country house fixtures during his university vacations. This gave him the chance to assess the form of many promising amateur players and he used his social contacts to good advantage in drumming up support for the county side.

His rising status in the affairs of Glamorgan CCC was confirmed in 1893, when the twenty-five year old took over as the county's treasurer. That summer, he also struck a cavalier 99 against Monmouthshire at the Arms Park and his middle-order strokeplay, combined with his athletic fielding and useful seam bowling, impressed many good judges. It seemed that the young gentleman was poised to play a leading role both on and off the field with Glamorgan, but within weeks of his innings of 99, Llewelyn had committed suicide. His funeral was attended by hundreds of people from the local gentry and sporting world, and all of the Glamorgan committee attended as a mark of respect to someone who they had seen as a future captain and administrator of the club.

Jim McConnon

RHB and OB, 1950-1961

Born: Burnopfield, 21 June 1922

Batting career:

M	I	NO	Runs	Av
243	350	38	4514	14.70

50	100	CT/ST
13	–	143

Bowling career:

O	M	R	W	Av
5913.2	1593	15656	799	19.59

5wI	10wM
49	12

Career best performances:
95 v Middlesex, Arms Park, 1958
8/36 v Nottinghamshire, Trent Bridge, 1953

Jim McConnon entered professional cricket in 1950 at the age of twenty-eight after a football career with Aston Villa and Welsh League clubs. Despite his late entry, McConnon soon established a regular place in the Glamorgan side as an off-spinner and, together with a high, flowing action, he utilised his long fingers to become a big spinner of the ball. In his second season of county cricket, he took 136 wickets, including 6/27 and a hat-trick in Glamorgan's victory over the 1951 Springboks at Swansea. This remarkable performance confirmed his abilities against Test-class batsmen, although even in this game at Swansea, McConnon had to be gently cajoled along by captain Wilf Wooller and wicketkeeper Haydn Davies.

After missing much of 1952 with a knee injury, McConnon returned to the side in 1953, finishing with 97 victims. His efforts did not go unnoticed by the England selectors and there was confirmation at the end of the season that he was a potential Test spinner with his selection in the Commonwealth touring party to India in 1953/54. He continued in good form in 1954, claiming 105 wickets, and was selected in the England side for two Tests against Pakistan. He began his Test career with a return of 3/12 from six overs, as well as four catches, and was duly included on the Ashes tour in 1954/55.

However, McConnon sustained a series of injuries while in Australia and a broken finger forced him to return home early. He never got another chance at Test level, but he continued to be a very effective spinner, taking 99 wickets in 1957 and 113 wickets at 18 apiece in 1959. By this time, he had also formed a successful partnership with Don Shepherd, as well as becoming a forceful late order batsman, and came within five runs of hitting a Championship hundred against Middlesex at the Arms Park in 1958.

McConnon took a benefit in 1961, but during the summer, he aggravated several old injuries and at the end of the season he retired from the first-class game.

Majid Khan

RHB and RM or OB, 1968-1976

Born: Ludhiana, India, 28 September 1946

Batting career:

M	I	NO	Runs	Av
154	270	17	9610	37.98
111	*110*	*6*	*2535*	*24.38*

50	100	CT/ST
47	21	155
16	*–*	*34*

Bowling career:

O	M	R	W	Av
723.3	216	1674	51	32.82
219.0	*33*	*676*	*35*	*19.31*

5wI	10wM
–	–

Career best performances:
204 v Surrey, The Oval, 1972
4/48 v Hampshire, Portsmouth, 1972
97 v Gloucestershire, Bristol, 1975*
5/24 v Northants, Northampton, 1969

Majid Khan was one of the first overseas Test stars to make a name for himself in county cricket and, during nine seasons with Glamorgan from 1968 until 1976, the graceful Pakistani scored over 9,000 runs and recorded 21 first-class centuries, besides leading the county from 1973.

The son of Dr Jahangir Khan, Majid played for Lahore from 1961/62, made his Test debut against Australia in 1964/65 and toured England with the 1967 Pakistanis. During the match with Glamorgan, the elegant batsman blasted a rapid 147 in 89 minutes, hitting Roger Davis for 5 sixes in an over. Wilf Wooller had been a close friend of Majid's father when he was at Cambridge and the influential Glamorgan secretary persuaded the committee to sign the dashing strokemaker.

He passed 1,000 runs in his first season with Glamorgan in 1968 and showed a priceless ability to bat on difficult wickets. Majid needed all his skill at Glamorgan's new Sophia Gardens ground, where there were problems with the new wicket. Many consider his finest innings to be his 156 out of 256 against Worcestershire in 1969. This great innings enabled Glamorgan to win the game and the County Championship title.

In autumn 1969, Majid went to Emmanuel College, where he won three Blues from 1970 until 1972 and led Cambridge to victory in the 1972 Varsity Match. Majid was appointed the Glamorgan captain in 1973 and on many occasions his team were very grateful for their leader's quick scoring, which helped give the bowlers plenty of time to bowl opponents out. In 1972 he won the Lawrence Trophy for making a century in 70 minutes against Warwickshire, while in the 1975 Sunday League match with Northamptonshire, Majid hit 50 off just 22 balls.

Sadly, Majid lost form in 1976 and he quit the county scene midway through the season, but he continued to play in Test cricket before retiring at the end of the 1982/83 series with New Zealand, having won 63 caps. In all first-class cricket, Majid Khan made 27,328 runs, hit 73 centuries and took 224 wickets. After retiring from professional cricket, Majid moved into broadcasting and became Controller of Sport for Pakistan Television. Recently he has served as chief executive of the Pakistani Cricket Board.

Austin Matthews
RHB and RFM, 1937-1947

Born: Penarth, 3 May 1904
Died: Llandudno, 29 July 1977

Batting career:

M	I	NO	Runs	Av
51	71	24	691	14.70

50	100	CT/ST
–	–	12

Bowling career:

O	M	R	W	Av
1473.1	353	3607	277	15.88

5wl	10wM
16	4

Career best performances:
37 v Essex, Chelmsford, 1946
7/12 v Somerset, Pontypridd, 1946

Austin Matthews played Test cricket barely three weeks after making his Glamorgan debut in 1937. His elevation followed an impressive spell of fast swing bowling against the New Zealanders and a return of 14/132 against Sussex on a perfect batting wicket at Hastings. He was drafted into the England side for the Third Test at The Oval and dismissed Walter Hadlee in both innings.

Matthews first emerged as a talented young sportsman in the mid-1920s and actually declined an offer to join Glamorgan in 1923 to carry on his college studies. He continued to play club cricket for Cardiff and rugby for Penarth.

The winter game initially had greater openings for Matthews. He won a place in a final Welsh trial and, after finishing his studies, he accepted an offer to join Northampton RFC.

While in the East Midlands, Matthews continued to play club cricket with success and made his first-class debut for Northamptonshire in 1927. The prospect of a lucrative career in cricket and the unlikely prospect of a Welsh rugby cap resulted in Matthews switching back to cricket and retiring from rugby. He duly became

Northamptonshire's regular opening bowler and, as befitted a strong rugby player, Matthews also developed into a fierce hitting lower-order batsman, making a career best 116 against Warwickshire at Edgbaston in 1929.

He continued to play for Northamptonshire until the end of 1936, when a difference of opinion over his new contract led to him leaving the club, and taking up coaching appointments at Cambridge University and Stowe School. At the end of the 1937 summer term, Matthews returned to Penarth and renewed his friendship with Maurice Turnbull. The Glamorgan skipper knew of Matthews's ability and, with some Glamorgan bowlers carrying injuries, Matthews agreed to turn out for Glamorgan. Barely two weeks later, he had an England cap as well!

This helped to refuel his appetite for county cricket and he continued to play for Glamorgan until 1947. Indeed, in 1946 he claimed a total of 88 wickets and continued to be almost unplayable in the right conditions, taking 7/12 against Somerset at Pontypridd and 9/23 during the match against Sussex at Horsham.

Matthew Maynard

RHB and RM, 1985-present

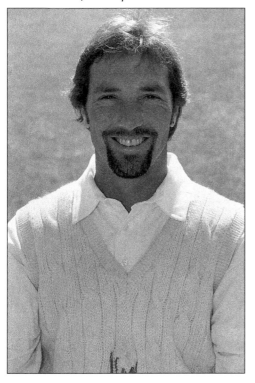

Born: Oldham, 21 March 1966

Batting career:

M	I	NO	Runs	Av
295	469	52	18146	43.65
184	*275*	*23*	*8765*	*34.78*

50	100	CT/ST
101	40	275/3
56	*10*	*113/1*

Bowling career:

O	M	R	W	Av
139.4	19	731	6	121.83
18.4	*0*	*110*	*1*	*110.00*

5wI	10wM
–	–

Career best performances:
243 v Hampshire, Southampton, 1991
3/21 v Oxford University, Oxford, 1987
151* v Middlesex, Lord's, 1996
v Durham, Darlington, 1991
1/13 v Somerset, Sophia Gardens, 1999

Matthew Maynard has been one of the most destructive batsman and successful captains in the club's history. He burst onto the county scene at Swansea in 1985 and scored an amazing century on his first-class debut (reaching his maiden hundred with three successive sixes off Yorkshire's Phil Carrick).

Maynard was born in Oldham and brought up at Menai Bridge in North Wales and, after a short spell on the Kent staff, he joined Glamorgan in 1985. Ever since, the bold right-handed batsman has thrilled the county's supporters with his dashing strokeplay and set a host of batting records. In 1986 he became the youngest ever Glamorgan player to score 1,000 runs and in 1987 he hit a breathtaking century before lunch against Somerset. He repeated the feat against Worcestershire in 1988 and further displays of such uninhibited batting drew the attention of England's selectors; Maynard made his Test debut against the West Indies at The Oval in August 1988. He only scored 3 and 10, but at the end of the summer he was

voted as the Young Cricketer of the Year. Maynard got a further taste of international cricket in 1989/90 as he toured South Africa with Mike Gatting's English XI.

The presence of Viv Richards in the Glamorgan side of 1990 helped Maynard to curb his impetuous instincts and a series of large hundreds soon followed. In 1991 he scored centuries in each innings against Gloucestershire, a double century against Nottinghamshire and, at the end of the summer, a career best 243 against Hampshire at Southampton. Maynard also gained invaluable experience in New Zealand playing for Northern Districts in 1990/91 and 1991/92, and in his first innings in New Zealand he also scored a century on his debut.

Maynard's quick scoring talents have also been a key feature behind Glamorgan's success in one-day cricket in the 1990s – in particular the Sunday League title in 1993. During that summer, Maynard also struck a century before lunch against the Australians at Neath and was recalled to the England side

Left: A straight drive from Matthew Maynard during Glamorgan's NatWest Trophy encounter with Durham at Sophia Gardens, Cardiff, in 1993. Right: *Matthew Maynard tickles the ball down the leg-side at Worcester during the Benson and Hedges Cup match against Worcestershire at New Road in May 1990.*

for two Tests in the Ashes series. He also won a place on the winter tour to the West Indies, where he won another Test cap and appeared in five one-day internationals.

By this time, Maynard had also tasted life as a county captain, leading Glamorgan during 1992 when Alan Butcher was injured. At the end of 1995, Maynard was appointed the county captain and, during his benefit year the following summer, Maynard began a vintage season by scoring the fastest ever century for Glamorgan in one-day cricket, with a hundred off just 58 balls against the British Universities. By the end of the season he had 1,610 runs to his name in first-class games at the healthy average of 61.62 and was included in England's squad for their one-day internationals against both India and Pakistan.

He was not too far away from the winter tour party, or even leading the England 'A' team to Australia, but Maynard put these disappointments behind him in 1997 by leading Glamorgan to their third Championship success and a semi-final place in the NatWest Trophy. Towards the end of the season, Maynard was in vintage form with the bat, scoring a scintillating 161* against Worcestershire and a breathtaking 142 against Somerset at Taunton. The latter was one of Maynard's finest innings and he remarkably reached his hundred without hitting a single.

Maynard was still at the helm in 2000, as Glamorgan progressed to the final of the Benson & Hedges Cup. In the semi-final victory over Surrey he played another match-winning innings, this time of 109.

Jack Mercer
RHB and RFM, 1922-1939

Born: Southwick, Sussex, 22 April 1893
Died: Westminster, 31 August 1987

Batting career:

M	I	NO	Runs	Av
412	578	100	5730	11.98

50	100	CT/ST
10	–	124

Bowling career:

O	M	R	W	Av
13813.5	3242	34058	1460	23.32

5wI	10wM
98	16

Career best performances:
72 v Surrey, The Oval, 1934
10/51 v Worcestershire, Worcester, 1936

Jack Mercer was a colourful, larger-than-life character who had a fine career as a swing bowler for Glamorgan, as well as briefly for Sussex and latterly Northamptonshire. Mercer is also the only Glamorgan bowler in the history of the club to take all ten wickets in an innings in a first-class match and he was the first bowler to take over 1,000 wickets for Glamorgan.

As a young man, Mercer had played club cricket in the Sussex area and been on the county's groundstaff before travelling across Europe to Russia. He also served with the Royal Sussex Regiment during the Great War, before settling down at the end of the war by opting for life as a professional cricketer. He played sporadically for Sussex between 1919 and 1921, but found his opportunities restricted by the presence of the legendary Maurice Tate.

In 1922 Mercer decided to move to South Wales and to qualify for Glamorgan. From 1924 he became their opening bowler, regularly claiming over 90 wickets in a season and, on 6 occasions, passing the 100 mark. Whilst these

are impressive statistics in their own right, Mercer's tally would have been much higher had Glamorgan had the services of more athletic fielders and agile catchers close to the wicket. Many times each season a greying and portly amateur would spill a catch in the slips, only for Mercer to say 'bad luck and well stopped, Sir' before ruefully returning to his bowling mark!

Mercer's success was based on the priceless ability to swing the ball either way and on unhelpful wickets he often reduced his pace and bowled off-cutters. This allowed Mercer to undertake long spells and, even in his forties, Mercer was always willing to shoulder the brunt of the bowling. Indeed, the finest moment of his career came (quite fittingly) in his benefit year in 1936, when the forty-one-year-old seamer took all ten wickets against Worcestershire, returning figures of 10/51. On that amazing day at the New Road ground, Mercer bowled an immaculate length and swung the ball lavishly in the humid atmosphere, and none of the Worcestershire batsmen played him with any

Left: *Jack Mercer in conversation before the start of play in Glamorgan's match against Somerset at Weston-Super-Mare in 1933.* Right: *Jack Mercer bowling at Swansea during a special demonstration in 1936.*

authority. After taking the first nine wickets to fall, all of the Glamorgan team realised that Mercer could take all ten, but several half-chances were spilled as the fielders desperately strove to help him create a piece of club history. Mercer's reward finally came as the Worcestershire's number eleven skied a ball into the outfield. George Lavis ran underneath it, juggled with the ball for a few heart-stopping moments, before safely holding on to give Mercer his tenth wicket.

Mercer was also a more-than-useful tail-end batsman, who during the course of his career played several explosive innings. On one occasion at Swansea, he played a remarkable firm-footed drive high out of the St Helen's ground, with the ball carrying across the Mumbles Road and into the entrance hall of the railway station alongside the beach. At Cardiff in 1939, he hit Dick Howarth of

Worcestershire for 31 runs in an eight ball over, with 4 sixes in 6 balls – all high into the rugby grandstand and clanging up against the metalwork.

These cavalier displays of batting reflected Mercer's happy-go-lucky outlook on life and he certainly lived life to the full. Indeed, it is said that he learned of his selection on the MCC tour to India and the Far East in 1926/27 whilst at Longchamp Racecourse in France. He was also a fine card player and a member of the Magic Circle.

After retiring from playing, he acted as coach and then scorer for Northamptonshire. Even when well into his seventies, the genial Mercer was able to pass on helpful tips to aspiring county bowlers. As for his own long career, he always attributed his stamina to walking as a young man across the South Downs for mile after mile.

Colin Metson
RHB and WK, 1987-1997

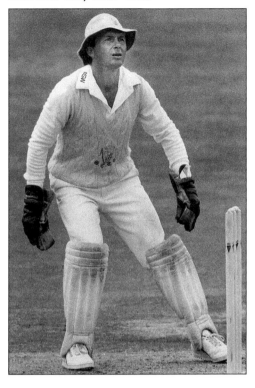

Born: Goffs Oak, Herts., 2 July 1963

Batting career:

M	I	NO	Runs	Av
207	271	62	3633	17.38
207	*117*	*43*	*873*	*11.80*

50	100	CT/ST
5	–	509/49
–	–	*200/52*

Bowling Career:

O	M	R	W	Av
1.0	1	0	0	–

5wI	10wM
–	–

Career best performances:
84 v Kent, Maidstone, 1991
30 v Hampshire, Bournemouth, 1990

Colin Metson was Glamorgan's wicketkeeper from 1987 until 1996, displaying flair and panache behind the stumps. His neat 'keeping made him a popular figure with Glamorgan fans who found it amazing that inferior wicketkeepers were often chosen for the England side.

He began his county career as Paul Downton's understudy at Middlesex from 1981, and with Downton in the England team, Metson proved to be a more than capable deputy. After finishing his studies, Metson showed a desire to play regular Championship cricket and an opportunity with Glamorgan came his way when Terry Davies decided to emigrate to Australia at the end of 1986. Metson accepted Glamorgan's offer, joined them at the start of the 1987 season and won a regular place for the next ten seasons.

His agile and quietly efficient wicketkeeping soon won high praise, with perhaps the most apt and eloquent coming from Alan Knott. The former England and Kent 'keeper once remarked 'how deceptive Colin Metson is as a wicketkeeper. He is very relaxed in everything he does, yet he has speed of movement like a cat. He also has amazing anticipation – even when standing up to the wicket he has moved away from the stumps to catch batsmen mis-hitting their sweep or reverse-sweep shots.'

In Glamorgan's NatWest Trophy quarter-final against Middlesex in 1995, Metson won the Man of the Match award after a top-class display of wicketkeeping. He also set a number of new wicketkeeping records for the club – including 7 catches in an innings against Derbyshire at Chesterfield in 1991 and twice taking 9 victims in a match (against Worcestershire at Worcester in 1993 and against Surrey at The Oval in 1995).

He was a competent lower-order batsman, often acting as the county's nightwatchman. In fact, he had also performed this job with Middlesex, for whom he hit a career best 96 against Gloucestershire at Uxbridge in 1984. Metson was awarded a benefit year by Glamorgan in 1997, during which he played his final game for the county, having lost his place to Adrian Shaw. He has continued to play for St Fagan's CC and the MCC, and leads Wales in the Minor County Championship in 2000.

Herbie Morgan

RHB and OB, 1889-1905

Born: Cardiff, December 1870
Died: Lower Penarth, 5 February 1933

Batting career:

M	I	NO	Runs	Av
(92	151	6	2831	19.52)

50	100	CT/ST
(9	4	67)

Bowling career:

O	M	R	W	Av
(40	8	129	7	18.43)

5wI	10wM
(–	–)

Career best performances:
(254 v Monmouthshire, Arms Park, 1901)
(3/50 v Wiltshire, Arms Park, 1894)

Herbie Morgan set several milestones with his batting for Glamorgan during the 1890s and 1900s. In 1890 he became their first batsman to record a century, whilst in 1901 he became their first double centurion in the Minor County fixture with Monmouthshire.

Morgan had first played for the county as an eighteen year old in their inaugural contest at Lord's in 1889 against the MCC, and he earned his place in the county side after some forthright innings for Penarth CC, for which he also became known as 'The Penarth Slogger'.

In 1890, Morgan hit Glamorgan's first ever hundred in their match with Monmouthshire at the Arms Park, although the nineteen year old only played when Daniel Jones dropped out of the original eleven on the morning of the match. Morgan was drafted in as a late replacement and, despite going in at number seven, he raced to a quickfire 147, with 4 sixes and 15 fours. He survived many chances as the Monmouthshire fielders spilled several chances in the deep.

Morgan's farming commitments prevented him from turning out on a regular basis, but he was still able to record centuries against the Surrey Second XI and Berkshire. His finest moment with the bat came in 1901, remarkably in his first innings of the summer for the county, as Morgan recorded the club's first double century: he amassed 254 out of the county's total of 538 against Monmouthshire, after the visitors had been initially handicapped by the late arrival of several players, following a train accident between Newport and Cardiff. Morgan then inflicted further embarrassment with a blistering display of hitting, with a solitary six and 40 fours, leaving some of the Monmouthshire players wishing that they had never turned up at all.

He failed to get past fifty in his other nine innings that summer, but he proved it was not a fluke by making a rapid 94 against Surrey at The Oval in 1902, followed by an aggressive 80 at the Arms Park against Devon. He eventually retired at the end of the 1905 season, but maintained his link with the county club by serving on the committee until 1909. In his youth, Morgan had also been a talented rugby player and had enjoyed a successful career with Penarth RFC.

J. Trevil Morgan

LHB, RM and occasional WK, 1925-1934

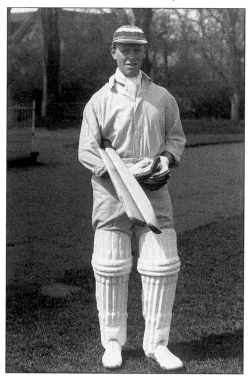

Born: Llandaff, 7 May 1907
Died: Clifton, 18 December 1976

Batting career:

M	I	NO	Runs	Av
39	52	3	792	16.16

50	100	CT/ST
2	1	9/2

Bowling career:

O	M	R	W	Av
168.5	32	535	11	48.63

5wI	10wM
–	–

Career best performances:
103* v South Africans, Swansea, 1929
3/16 v Warwickshire, Edgbaston, 1933

J. Trevil Morgan was a member of the famous family who owned and managed the drapery store in Cardiff, which developed into one of the city's finest department stores. In fact, his commitments with the family business prevented him from commanding a regular place in Glamorgan's First XI either side of the Second World War. Even so, he still became a highly successful captain of the county's Second XI, who played in the Minor County Championship from 1935 until 1937 and again between 1948 and 1950. Under his astute captaincy, many young players flourished before going on to even better things in the County Championship.

Educated at Charterhouse, Morgan was a left-handed batsman and right-arm medium-pace bowler, who also kept wicket on several occasions for the county. He made his Glamorgan debut in 1925, before going to Cambridge where he won Blues in 1928, 1929 and 1930, and played alongside Maurice Turnbull. During 1929 he hit an impressive century for Glamorgan against the South Africans, with 2 sixes and 11 fours, displaying great composure and flair against the Springbok bowlers. The 1929 season had been highly productive while he was at Cambridge, as he compiled a stylish 149 in the Varsity Match. He was also the first wicketkeeper to achieve this feat and he owed his place in the record books to his friend Turnbull, who had shown great faith in Morgan's ability behind the stumps.

In 1930, Morgan successfully led the Cambridge side in the Varsity Match, winning wide acclaim for setting Oxford a target of 307 in around two and a half hours and then bowling them out for 101. However, Morgan shrugged off the plaudits with typical modesty, claiming that he had only declared because he thought it indecent to go on batting, and he had never given any thought that Oxford would either go for the runs or get themselves out! After leaving university, he returned to South Wales to join the family business. Judging by his fine form for both Cambridge and Glamorgan, Morgan would have become a highly successful county batsman had he been able to play Championship cricket on a regular basis during the 1930s.

Hugh Morris

LHB and OB, 1981-1997

Born: Cardiff, 5 October 1963

Batting career:

M	I	NO	Runs	Av
289	502	51	18520	41.06
263	*256*	*26*	*8169*	*35.52*

50	100	CT/ST
88	52	175
46	*13*	*91*

Bowling career:

O	M	R	W	Av
58	6	380	2	190.00
5	*0*	*27*	*1*	*27.00*

5wI	10wM
–	–

Career best performances:
233* v Warwickshire, Sophia Gardens, 1997
1/6 v Oxford University, The Parks, 1987
154 v Staffordshire, Sophia Gardens, 1989*
1/14 v Combined Univs, Sophia Gardens, 1988

Hugh Morris maintained the tradition for high quality, left-handed opening batsmen, established by Emrys Davies and Alan Jones, and it was fitting that in Morris's final match for the county in 1997, he equalled Jones's record for the number of centuries in first-class cricket for the Welsh county. Indeed, Morris was one of the most consistent and dependable batsmen on the county circuit in the 1980s and 1990s, and it was no coincidence that Glamorgan enjoyed the most successful period ever in their history when Morris was opening their innings.

Morris had made his county debut in 1981 whilst still at Blundell's School, where he set a host of batting records. After playing for, and captaining, Young England during the mid-1980s, he became Glamorgan's youngest-ever leader in 1986. He only had a brief period in charge initially, as he stood down from the captaincy at the end of the 1989 season in order to concentrate on his batting – this

was a move which reaped its rewards in 1990 as he established a new club record of 10 centuries and 2,276 runs, and together with fellow left-hander Alan Butcher, the Glamorgan openers became the most productive pairing in Championship cricket.

During 1991 the plucky left-hander also had a brief taste of Test cricket, playing against the West Indies and Sri Lanka. In the Fifth Test at The Oval, Morris bravely fended off the hostile West Indian pace attack to make 44 in a partnership of 112 with Graham Gooch. Yet at the end of the summer, the England selectors opted for other openers – with inferior records – and Morris acted as captain of the 'A' tour to the West Indies. He fulfilled this role again in 1993/94 to South Africa and, despite Morris's consistent form at county level, he only won 3 Test caps.

Morris returned to the Glamorgan captaincy in 1993 and led Glamorgan to the Sunday League title, proudly lifting the

Left: *Hugh Morris sweeps against Middlesex at Colwyn Bay in 1995.* Right: *Hugh Morris cover drives for England against the Sri Lankans at Lord's in 1991.*

AXA Trophy after Glamorgan had defeated Kent, their nearest challengers, in a head-to-head contest in the final game of the season at Canterbury. At the end of the 1995 season, he handed over the reins to Matthew Maynard and continued to be a prolific opener with his new partner Steve James. In May 1996, he hit 202 against Yorkshire in the opening match of the season and repeated the feat in the first game of 1997, recording a career best 233* against Warwickshire at Cardiff. It was an innings of the highest class, but it ended in unusual circumstances as Hugh ducked into a ferocious short ball from Allan Donald, the South African fast bowler. Morris was helped off the field, but fortunately there was no lasting damage and he quickly regained his place in the Glamorgan side.

Hugh's final season of county cricket proved to be in 1997 and he ended his playing career on a high note as Glamorgan won the Championship; in his final game at Taunton, Hugh hit 165 to equal Alan Jones's record of 52 centuries in first-class cricket. With 13 centuries in other games, Hugh has scored more hundreds for Glamorgan than any other batsman and his first-class aggregate of 18,520 runs places him in fourth place in the county's all-time list of run-scorers.

He retired at the end of the 1997 season to take up the post of technical coaching director with the ECB and has subsequently been instrumental in overseeing many important changes and introducing new coaching initiatives.

Ezra Moseley

RHB and RF, 1980-1986

Born: Barbados, 5 January 1958

Batting career:

M	I	NO	Runs	Av
35	43	10	655	19.85
29	*19*	*6*	*107*	*8.23*

50	100	CT/ST
4	–	7
–	–	*3*

Bowling career:

O	M	R	W	Av
910.1	195	2729	114	23.94
208.1	*33*	*666*	*35*	*19.03*

5wI	10wM
5	–

Career best performances:
70* v Kent, Canterbury, 1980
6/23 v Australians, Swansea, 1986
25 v Essex, Chelmsford, 1986
4/8 v Kent, Sophia Gardens, 1981

Ezra Moseley, with 114 victims, is one of only two overseas bowlers to take over 100 first-class wickets during their careers with Glamorgan. Had it not been for a serious injury, Moseley would surely have been the club's most successful overseas bowler, not to mention one of the best fast bowlers in county cricket.

Moseley joined Glamorgan in 1980 as a raw twenty-two year old who had impressed in club cricket in his native Barbados, but had no first-class experience. Even so, the fiery fast bowler burst onto the county scene, taking seven wickets on his Championship debut on a slow Swansea wicket. Moseley ended the season with 51 victims to his name and he consolidated on this headway the following season with a further 52 at just 18 apiece, with a hat-trick against Kent in their Benson & Hedges Cup match in 1981. However, his finest performance in 1981 came again at Swansea, where he took 6/23 against the Australian tourists and, despite the sluggish wicket, confirmed his ability to trouble Test-class batsmen with his speed and swerve through the air.

Just when critics were predicting a bright future for the West Indian, he broke down in 1982 with a stress fracture in his back, which required surgery and a long spell on the sidelines. With uncertain medical reports over his long-term future, Glamorgan were forced to hire Winston Davis, another West Indian quickie, as Moseley's replacement. After plenty of rest, he modified his action and run-up, and returned to the UK as a professional in the Lancashire Leagues. He also went on 'rebel' West Indian tours to South Africa, as well as appearing for Eastern Province, where his skidding pace off a relatively short run, made him a hostile bowler.

In 1986 Moseley briefly reappeared for the Welsh county, following an injury to Javed Miandad, and in 1990 he turned down an offer from Surrey to be their overseas player, preferring instead to continue as a professional in the Lancashire Leagues. By this time, Moseley had also become a Test cricketer and, between 1989/90 and 1990/91, he played in 2 Tests and 9 one-day internationals for the West Indies.

Len Muncer

RHB and LB or OB, 1947-1954

Born: Hampstead, 23 October 1913
Died: Camden, 18 January 1982

Batting career:

M	I	NO	Runs	Av
224	333	46	6460	22.50

50	100	CT/ST
21	4	111

Bowling career:

O	M	R	W	Av
6642.2	1807	14462	708	20.42

5wI	10wM
42	8

Career best performances:
135 v Somerset, Swansea, 1952
9/62 v Essex, Brentwood, 1948

Len Muncer was a key member of Glamorgan's victorious team in the 1948 Championship. The off-spinner had made his Glamorgan debut the previous year, having moved to South Wales after a thirteen-year spell on Middlesex's books, primarily as a leg-spinner. He had failed to command a regular place in the Middlesex XI, and with Johnnie Clay going into semi-retirement, Wilf Wooller persuaded Muncer to join the Welsh county and concentrate on off-spin. He soon repaid Wooller for his advice by taking 107 wickets in 1947, including returns of 8/36 against Gloucestershire at Cheltenham and 9/97 against Surrey at the Arms Park.

He followed this with 156 victims in the Championship summer of 1948, including a career best match haul of 15/201 in the game against Sussex at Swansea. He also took 9/62 against Essex at Brentwood and in the course of the innings could easily have equalled Jack Mercer's record of taking all ten wickets. After claiming the first eight on a rain-affected wicket, Muncer must have thought he was in with a chance of the record. However, he selflessly held onto a sharp chance at slip, off Willie Jones's bowling, before picking up the final wicket of Essex's second innings and his ninth of the innings to finish with match figures of 15/161.

His fine close catching was a valuable asset and in 1948 Muncer took 31 catches at slip or in the leg trap. He also proved to be an aggressive middle-order batsman, scoring over 500 runs in every season with Glamorgan. In 1951 Muncer performed the match double of 107* and 10/57 against Derbyshire at Chesterfield, whilst in the 1952 season he achieved the seasonal double of 100 wickets and 1,076 runs.

Whilst serving with the Sherwood Foresters in the Second World War, Sergeant Muncer had been a POW in Southeast Asia, including a spell working on the Burma-Siam Railway. This hard work started to tell, as Muncer picked up a groin strain in 1953 and after taking a benefit in 1954, he announced his retirement from first-class cricket with 8,645 runs and 755 wickets at 20.90. He took up a coaching post at Lord's, served as head coach until 1977 and recommended many young cricketers to Glamorgan.

Jack Nash

RHB and RM or OB, 1900-1922

Born: Blean, Kent, 18 September 1873
Died: Battersea, 6 December 1956

Batting career:

M	I	NO	Runs	Av
36	65	9	315	5.62
(123	158	35	958	8.01)

50	100	CT/ST
–	–	6
(–	–	92)

Bowling career:

O	M	R	W	Av
1218.0	360	2901	133	21.81
(3620.0	1172	8607	604	14.25)

5wI	10wM
11	2

Career best performances:
28 v Derbyshire, Chesterfield, 1921
9/93 v Sussex, Swansea, 1922
(44 v Monmouthshire, Arms Park, 1908)
(8/31 v Devon, Exeter, 1904)

'Jack' Nash was a stalwart member of Glamorgan's Minor County side and his tricky combination of seam and off-spin helped the club to their early successes and first-class status. He was still in the team during their inaugural Championship season at the age of forty-seven.

Nash had joined Cardiff CC as their professional and groundsman in 1900, and he made his debut for the Glamorgan side against the MCC at the Arms Park later that season. He quickly became a regular in the side, bearing the brunt of the bowling and returning some fine figures, including 12/77 in the 1903 match against Berkshire, whilst in 1908 he took 9/33 against the Oxford Harlequins at the Arms Park.

His accurate bowling and powers of spin were one of the reasons why Glamorgan did well in Minor County cricket at this time and it was a huge blow when Nash moved to Haslington in the Lancashire Leagues in 1911. The following season he joined Uddingston in Glasgow, where he stayed until 1919. But then, with Glamorgan poised to become a first-class side, Nash returned to South Wales and joined Neath CC.

In 1921 he returned to Cardiff CC and achieved his long held ambition of playing first-class cricket as Glamorgan entered the County Championship. In the opening game of the season, he returned the figures of 29-11-45-4 as Sussex were defeated at the Arms Park. He also proved he had lost none of his guile by taking 6/37 against Leicestershire, before tormenting the Worcestershire batsmen – in the match at Kidderminster he took 6/66 and 4/76, before taking 7/34 and 8/82 in the return match at Swansea, fully exploiting a dry, dusty wicket as Glamorgan defeated the visitors.

In 1922 he had another outstanding match at Swansea, returning career best figures of 9/93 against Sussex. But by mid-summer, age had finally caught up with the forty-eight-year-old spinner, as he only took one other five-wicket haul in the second half of the season. He retired from county cricket at the end of 1922, but continued to play for Cardiff CC. He tended the Arms Park wicket until 1926, when he joined the first-class umpires list. Nash stood in 104 games until leaving the first-class scene in 1930.

Malcolm Nash
LHB and LM, 1966-1983

| Born: Abergavenny, 9 May 1945 |

Batting career:

M	I	NO	Runs	Av
335	467	67	7120	17.81
266	*223*	*41*	*2244*	*12.33*

50	100	CT/ST
25	2	148
4	*1*	*47*

Bowling career:

O	M	R	W	Av
9193.3	2426	25601	991	25.83
2034.5	*358*	*6767*	*320*	*21.15*

5wI	10wM
45	5

Career best performances:
130 v Surrey, The Oval, 1976
9/56 v Hampshire, Basingstoke, 1975
6/29 v Worcestershire, Worcester, 1975
103 v Hampshire, Swansea, 1976*

Malcolm Nash will always be remembered as the bowler struck by Sir Garfield Sobers for 6 sixes in an over during the match with Nottinghamshire at Swansea in 1968. But what is often forgotten is that Nash was not bowling in his usual style, but was experimenting with slow left-arm spin as the visitors approached a declaration.

Tall and lean, Malcolm Nash was a lively left-arm seam bowler whose left-arm over the wicket bowling made him one of the best new ball bowlers in county cricket during the 1970s. Indeed, Nash was rated by Barry Richards, the legendary Springbok batsman, as one of the most difficult bowlers with the new ball that he faced whilst playing county cricket with Hampshire. Nash owed his success as a left-arm seamer to the knack of being able to move the ball both ways. Visiting batsmen were therefore unsure whether the ball would swing in or out and Nash invariably dismissed several top order batsmen when the shine was on the ball.

He was also a highly effective and miserly bowler in limited-over games, and frequently delivered his allocation of eight overs in the Sunday League straight through and at a minimal cost. Indeed, Nash still holds the record for the most economical spell for the Welsh county, returning figures of 8-4-8-1 and 8-4-8-2 against Lancashire in 1973 and 1980.

Nash was also a swashbuckling tail-end batsman and in 1976 he scored a century before lunch off just 61 balls, against Surrey at The Oval. In 1976 he became Glamorgan's first centurion in the Benson & Hedges competition, with 103* against Hampshire at Swansea, and in 1970 won the award for the fastest televised fifty in the Sunday League, after a half-century off 33 balls against Kent at Swansea.

In 1975 he also took a hat-trick against Worcestershire in the Sunday League and was chosen for the 1976 Test trial. According to John Arlott, 'if he had been a yard or two faster than his steady medium, his accuracy, movement, variety and intelligence would surely have given him a permanent England place'. Nash led Glamorgan in 1980 and 1981, before retiring at the end of the 1983 season with a total of 991 first-class wickets for Glamorgan.

Rodney Ontong

RHB and RM or OB, 1975-1989

Born: Johannesburg, 9 September 1955

Batting career:

M	I	NO	Runs	Av
257	413	65	10825	31.11
224	*199*	*29*	*4364*	*25.67*

50	100	CT/ST
53	18	116
18	*1*	*70*

Bowling career:

O	M	R	W	Av
5709.0	1277	17279	531	32.54
1528.4	*139*	*6308*	*199*	*31.70*

5wI	10wM
20	4

Career best performances:
204* v Middlesex, Swansea, 1984
8/67 v Nottinghamshire, Trent Bridge, 1985
100 v Northants, Abergavenny, 1982
5/30 v Somerset, Taunton,1985

Rodney Ontong was a gifted all-rounder, who led Glamorgan between 1984 and 1986, and had it not been for a horrific car crash which ended his professional career, Ontong might have won Test honours with England as a combative batsman and astute off-spinner.

Ontong had initially come over to the United Kingdom in the early 1970s to have football trials with Chelsea. He subsequently joined the MCC groundstaff, along with other talented young cricketers such as Ian Botham, and was recommended to Glamorgan by MCC coach Len Muncer. Ontong duly secured a contract with the Welsh county and made his first-class debut against the 1975 Australians.

Ontong spent a couple of years qualifying as an English player, before winning a regular place in the side in 1977 as a brisk medium-pace bowler and stylish middle-order batsman. His all-round skills proved invaluable to Glamorgan, as they enjoyed their best ever season in one-day cricket by reaching the Gillette Cup final.

During the early 1980s, Ontong moved up the batting order to number three and in 1983 he also changed bowling styles from pace to spin. He proved to be a big spinner of the ball and claimed 74 wickets in 1984, followed by 64 victims in 1985. During the 1985 season, he also produced one of the best ever all-round performances for Glamorgan, scoring 130 runs and returning figures of 13/106 against Nottinghamshire at Trent Bridge.

Ontong took over the Glamorgan captaincy midway through the 1984 season and, following his outstanding returns, his name was mentioned in high circles as a potential England all-rounder. He had previously turned down the opportunity of playing for the South African national side in the hope of playing for his adopted country. In 1987 he was asked about his availability for the World Cup, but was not in the final squad. Higher honours never came his way as his fine county career came to an abrupt end in August 1988 when he badly injured his knee in a motorway accident en route from Essex to Northamptonshire. Since retiring, Ontong has coached in South Africa for Northern Transvaal and is currently director of coaching for Gauteng.

Gilbert Parkhouse
RHB and RM, 1948-1964

Born: Swansea, 12 October 1925

Batting career:

M	I	NO	Runs	Av
435	759	48	22619	31.81
1	*1*	*0*	*17*	*17.00*

50	100	CT/ST
123	32	312
–	–	*1*

Bowling career:

O	M	R	W	Av
37.1	8	125	2	62.50

5wI 10wM

– –

Career best performances:
201 v Kent, Swansea, 1956
1/4 v Surrey, Llanelli, 1952
17 v Essex, Neath, 1964

Gilbert Parkhouse was perhaps the most graceful of any Welsh-born batsmen to play for Glamorgan. Born in Swansea and educated at Wycliffe College, he shone as a schoolboy sportsman and was offered trials by Gloucestershire CCC. However, Gilbert had his roots in Swansea and had spent hour after hour as a schoolboy in the nets at St Helen's being coached by that most loyal of Welsh sportsmen, Billy Bancroft. It was, therefore, not surprising that Gilbert opted to play cricket for Glamorgan and he is currently the only Glamorgan batsman to have scored Championship centuries against every first-class county. Indeed, it was fitting that he achieved this feat in May 1960 with 121 against Leicestershire on his home ground at St Helen's.

After appearing in wartime friendlies and completing his National Service, Gilbert made his long awaited debut for the Welsh county in 1948. He soon showed class with the bat, amassing over 1,200 runs in his debut season. Despite being slightly built, the youngster reeled off a wide range of forcing strokes and became an immaculate timer of the ball. He also developed into a safe fielder in the slips and was deservedly given his county cap at the end of the Championship season.

Parkhouse moved up from number three to partner opener Emrys Davies in 1950 and they shared a partnership of 241 against Somerset at Swansea, as well as 233 against Surrey at Swansea. During the summer, Parkhouse produced some elegant displays of batting, equally at home against the fast bowlers and the slower spinners. His excellent run of form also resulted in his selection for England in the Test series against the 1950 West Indians. During the summer he scored 1,742 runs, including three consecutive hundreds, and his fine form was rewarded with a place on the England tour to Australia and New Zealand. However, Gilbert struggled with poor health down under and failed to compete with Hutton, Washbrook, Edrich and Compton for a Test

Gilbert Parkhouse pulls Essex's Ray Smith for four at Ilford in 1949.

place. Although he played in three Tests, he never really gave a proper account of his true abilities during the tour.

It highlighted the rich vein of batting talent that the England selectors were able to ignore the claims of the phlegmatic Parkhouse and all despite him clocking up over 1,000 runs season after season.

Indeed, it was only whilst amassing a club record 2,071 runs in 1959 that the Welshman was recalled to the England side for the Third and Fourth Tests against India, and then after sharing an opening partnership of 146, he was omitted for the Fifth Test. Had the selectors shown more faith in him and capped him more than seven times, Parkhouse could have made a huge impact at Test level.

Parkhouse continued to play for Glamorgan until 1964 when, after some niggling back injuries, he retired from county cricket and took up a post as coach with Worcestershire and then Stewarts-Melville College in Edinburgh from 1966 until 1987.

A caricature of Gilbert Parkhouse, drawn by Mickey Durling in 1950.

Frank Pinch
RHB and RM, 1920-1926

Born: Bodmin, 24 February 1891
Died: Ashford, 8 October 1961
Batting career:

M	I	NO	Runs	Av
41	72	5	1068	15.94
(6	7	0	184	26.69)

50	100	CT/ST
2	1	24
(–	1	2)

Bowling career:

O	M	R	W	Av
402.0	84	1233	37	33.32
(144.2	47	360	30	12.00)

5wI	10wM
–	–

Career best performances:
138* v Worcestershire, Swansea, 1921
4/48 v Sussex, Arms Park, 1923
(109 v Wiltshire, Marlborough, 1920)
(4/9 v Wiltshire, Arms Park, 1920)

In 1921 Frank Pinch etched his name into the Glamorgan record books by scoring a century on his first-class debut for the Welsh county. The Cornish-born batsman struck an unbeaten 138* against Worcestershire at St Helen's in his maiden County Championship innings, in Glamorgan's inaugural season as a first-class county. It was not until 1985 that the feat was repeated by Matthew Maynard on his Glamorgan debut against Yorkshire. Pinch had played in six games during 1920 for Glamorgan in the Welsh county's final season as a Minor County and scored a century against Wiltshire at Marlborough. So, unlike Maynard, his century against Worcestershire was not his first major innings for the club.

Pinch had first come to the attention of the Glamorgan selectors before the Great War as a free scoring batsman and useful right-arm seam bowler for Barry Cricket and Athletic Club. After the war, he completed a teaching diploma and moved to the Home Counties. Despite teaching in Kent, Pinch retained his links with the Glamorgan officials and appeared during his school holidays in 1920. The following summer, he recorded his maiden century at Swansea in July 1921 as he shared an unbroken partnership of 195 for the sixth wicket with fellow schoolmaster George Cording. They had come to the wicket late on the first afternoon, after rain had interrupted play. The instructions from Glamorgan captain Norman Riches the next morning were to go for quick runs and the two teachers flayed the Worcestershire bowling to both record their one and only first-class hundred – surely a unique occurrence for the teaching profession!

Remarkably, the stylish amateur only scored two more half-centuries in 40 subsequent appearances, with 55 against the 1923 West Indians and 64 against Warwickshire at Edgbaston in August 1924. Even so, he continued to be a heavy scorer in club cricket, as well as playing for Wales in 1924 and for Sir Julian Cahn's XI in 1927 and 1928.

Mike Powell

Born: Abergavenny, 3 February 1977

Batting career:

M	I	NO	Runs	Av
37	61	10	2186	42.86
34	*32*	*3*	*549*	*18.93*

50	100	CT/ST
10	4	16
1	*–*	*9*

Bowling career:

O	M	R	W	Av
21.2	1	111	2	55.50

5wI	10wM
–	–

Career best performances:
200* v Oxford University, Oxford, 1997
2/39 v Oxford University, Oxford, 1999
55 v Derbyshire, Sophia Gardens, 1998

Mike Powell is a member of a well-known cricketing family from Abergavenny and he has the potential to become the mainstay of Glamorgan's middle order in the next decade.

Indeed, the solid right-handed batsman confirmed his rich potential with an innings of 200* on his first-class debut against Oxford University. By doing so he became only the third Englishman in the twentieth century to score a double hundred on their first-class debut – a feat previously achieved by Hubert Doggart for Cambridge University against Lancashire at Fenner's in 1948 and by Northamptonshire's David Sales, who scored 210* against Worcestershire at Kidderminster in 1996.

Powell's 200* was also the highest ever score on debut for Glamorgan, beating the 138* made by Frank Pinch. Powell, at 20 years and 95 days old, also became Glamorgan's youngest ever double centurion, beating John Hopkins (who had made 230 against Worcestershire in 1977 aged 24 years and 30 days).

The talented youngster from Crickhowell School made his Second XI debut for Glamorgan in 1996 and, after spending the off-season in Australia, began the 1997 season in impressive form with four hundreds in the opening five games for the Second XI and finished the season with a record aggregate of 1,210 runs.

Powell got further opportunities at first-team level following Hugh Morris's retirement at the end of 1997 and Tony Cottey's decision to join Sussex for 1999. During 1998, he struck his maiden Championship hundred at Northampton and in 1999 he was the county's leading run-scorer in first-class cricket. During the season he hit two further centuries, including an innings of 164 against Nottinghamshire at Colwyn Bay, during which he shared a partnership of 281 for the third wicket with Steve James. He came close to selection for the England 'A' tour to Bangladesh and New Zealand in 1999/2000 and in May 2000 the talented young Welshman proved that he has a big match temperament by making an impressive 67 during the victory over Surrey in the semi-final of the Benson & Hedges Cup.

Jim Pressdee
RHB and SLA, 1949-1965

Born: Mumbles, 19 June 1933

Batting career:

M	I	NO	Runs	Av
322	543	83	13411	29.16
6	*6*	*0*	*105*	*17.50*

50	100	CT/ST
75	12	344
1	*–*	*2*

Bowling career:

O	M	R	W	Av
3666.2	1095	8988	405	22.18
14.0	*4*	*101*	*3*	*33.67*

5wI	10wM
19	5

Career best performances:
150* v Cambridge University, Pontypridd, 1965
9/43 v Yorkshire, Swansea, 1965
60 v Essex, Neath, 1964
3/46 v Somerset, Arms Park, 1963

Jim Pressdee was one of the best all-rounders in Glamorgan's history. He became the club's youngest post-war cricketer in 1949, making his debut against Nottinghamshire at the Arms Park aged 16 years and 59 days. He was also a very talented schoolboy footballer, winning Welsh youth caps and playing for Swansea Town. But cricket held sway and Pressdee turned down the opportunity to represent Great Britain Youth against their West German counterparts at Wembley as he was selected to play for Glamorgan Second XI at Worcester!

After completing his National Service, Pressdee developed into an aggressive batsman and a clever spinner, who formed a useful attack with Don Shepherd and Jim McConnon. In 1959 Pressdee moved up to number three and recorded his maiden century, against India at the Arms Park. His score of 113, with a six and 15 fours, was even more impressive as it was made in Glamorgan's modest total of 182, with the next highest score being 19 from Alan Jones.

He continued in a rich vein of form over the next couple of years, amassing 1,892 runs in

1961, before compiling a career best 1,911 runs in 1962. Pressdee also had a rather perverse streak in his character, as testified by a century in 1961 before lunch on the final day of the game with Sussex, when Glamorgan were trying to save the match and other batsmen were opting for more sedate crease occupation.

Whilst his batting went from strength to strength, Pressdee rather lost confidence as a bowler and he only regained his self-belief after some useful spells in South Africa. Between 1959 and 1962, Pressdee had claimed just five wickets, but he returned to form in a remarkable way during 1963 with 104 wickets to complete the double. The following year he claimed 97 wickets and played a leading role in the famous victory over the 1964 Australians at Swansea.

In 1965 Pressdee claimed a career best 9/43 against Yorkshire at Swansea, but at the end of the summer, his career with Glamorgan came to an abrupt halt when, after several run-ins with the administration, Pressdee announced that he was emigrating to South Africa, where he played for North-East Transvaal until 1969/70.

Alan Rees

RHB and RM, 1955-1972

Born: Port Talbot, 17 February 1938
Died: Swansea, 3 March 1959

Batting career:

M	I	NO	Runs	Av
216	372	53	7681	24.07
17	*15*	*1*	*207*	*14.79*

50	100	CT/ST
36	2	113
1	*–*	*5*

Bowling career:

O	M	R	W	Av
94.3	11	398	6	66.33
1.0	*0*	*2*	*0*	*–*

5wl	10wM
–	–

Career best performances:
111* v Lancashire, Arms Park, 1964
3/68 v Kent, Arms Park, 1960
50 v Essex, Neath, 1964

Alan Rees was amongst the finest fielders in first-class cricket during the 1960s. He was a live-wire at cover point and his athletic fielding resulted in many dismissals. Rees joined the Glamorgan staff in the mid-1950s as a right-handed batsman and seam bowler, and he established a regular place in the middle order towards the end of the decade, after completing his studies at Loughborough University.

He won his county cap in 1963 and had his most productive season in 1964, when he scored 1,206 runs in first-class cricket. His tally included two centuries in consecutive matches, starting with 106* in the second innings of the match against Kent at Maidstone. He had joined Jim Pressdee at the crease when there were still 18 runs needed to avoid an innings defeat. The pair remained calm and unflustered for the next three hours, with Rees going on to register a stylish century, before making 111* in the following match against Lancashire at the Arms Park.

Rees's swift and athletic fielding was also highly regarded and in 1964 he was called up by the England selectors to act as a substitute fielder in the Third Test against Australia at Headingley. Rees was also a talented rugby player, appearing as fly-half for Maesteg, Aberavon, Leicester and Llanelli, and in 1962 he won three Welsh caps, playing against England, Scotland and France. At the end of the 1962 season, Rees opted to play Rugby League for Leeds RLFC and he turned professional.

Even so, he continued to play for Glamorgan during the summer months and in 1965 he achieved notoriety for being dismissed 'handled the ball' in Glamorgan's second innings against Middlesex at Lord's. He retired from first-class cricket in 1968, although he continued to play club cricket in the South Wales Cricket Association, reappeared in Gillette Cup matches for Glamorgan in 1970 and 1971, and in Sunday League games in 1972.

Gwyn Richards
RHB and OB, 1971-1979

Born: Maesteg, 29 November 1951

Batting career:

M	I	NO	Runs	Av
107	174	26	3370	22.77
96	*83*	*17*	*1058*	*16.03*

50	100	CT/ST
15	1	36
2	*2*	*25*

Bowling career:

O	M	R	W	Av
691.3	135	2257	48	47.02
287.2	*24*	*1213*	*45*	*26.96*

5wI	10wM
1	–

Career best performances:
102* v Yorkshire, Middlesborough, 1976
5/55 v Somerset, Taunton, 1978
73 v Gloucestershire, Sophia Gardens, 1978
5/29 v Lancashire, Swansea, 1977

Gwyn Richards was a key member of Glamorgan's team that reached the final of the Gillette Cup in 1977. The off-spinner bowled several accurate spells during the competition, especially in the semi-final at Swansea, where Richards returned figures of 12-4-17-2. He later shared a useful partnership with wicketkeeper Eifion Jones, which saw Glamorgan to victory with fifteen balls to go and gave the county a place in a major one-day final for the first time in the team's history. Richards also bowled an excellent containing spell in the final against Middlesex, conceding just 23 runs from his 12-over allocation, as well as taking the wicket of Graham Barlow.

Richards made his first-class debut for Glamorgan in 1971 whilst still on the MCC groundstaff and he showed promise as a middle-order batsman. He won a regular place in the side in 1974, but only scored a single half-century in 28 innings. After a series of good performances in the Second XI during 1975, Richards returned to the First XI in 1976 a more confident and assured batsman. This was confirmed by a maiden century against Yorkshire and he won his county cap at the end of the season, after making 774 runs in first-class cricket, as well as playing some promising innings in one-day games.

He continued to make some useful contributions in one-day matches in 1977, but he subsequently lost form and confidence in 1978, and left the county's staff during the following season. His career average might look a modest one, but without his efforts with bat and ball in 1977, Glamorgan might never have made it to their first one-day final at Lord's.

Viv Richards
RHB and RM or OB, 1990-1993

Born: Antigua, 7 March 1952

Batting career:

M	I	NO	Runs	Av
49	83	11	3382	46.97
60	*58*	*10*	*1921*	*40.02*

50	100	CT/ST
14	10	43
10	*2*	*27*

Bowling career:

O	M	R	W	Av
233.0	46	695	9	77.33
310.2	*15*	*1415*	*53*	*26.70*

5wI	10wM
–	–

Career best performances:
224* v Middlesex, Sophia Gardens, 1990
3/22 v Yorkshire, Sophia Gardens, 1993
109 v Derbyshire, Pontypridd, 1992
3/38 v Hampshire, Southampton, 1990

Sir Viv Richards, the legendary West Indian batsman, was an integral member of Glamorgan's side which won the AXA Sunday League in 1993. The forty-one-year-old 'Master Blaster' was in his final season of county cricket, but he excelled in the field and played several cameo innings with the bat. Indeed, the presence of Richards boosted the confidence of Hugh Morris's team and helped the youngsters to believe in their abilities. Perhaps it was no coincidence that the past ten years have been amongst the club's most successful in both Championship cricket and limited-overs games.

Richards played for the county in 1990, 1992 and 1993 and, despite being in the twilight of his career, he scored 12 centuries in first-class and one-day matches. His most prolific season was 1993 as he made 162* against Oxfordshire in the NatWest Trophy at Swansea, before sharing a partnership of 425 for the fourth wicket with Adrian Dale against Middlesex at Sophia Gardens whilst making an unbeaten 224. His score against Oxfordshire is still the highest individual innings in one-day cricket for Glamorgan, whilst his partnership with Dale is the highest for any wicket in the club's history.

His finest innings for Glamorgan came in the Championship match at Southampton in 1990. Hampshire had set a target of 364 off 102 overs, and after slumping to 139-5 with 42 overs remaining, a Glamorgan victory looked out of the question. But the West Indian had other ideas and, with the support of Nigel Cowley and Colin Metson, Richards turned the game around in Glamorgan's favour with a stunning, and at times savage attack, on the tiring Hampshire bowlers. In the final over Colin Metson scrambled a single off Malcolm Marshall's first delivery, before Richards hit 4, 6 and 4 to see Glamorgan to victory with 2 balls to spare.

Richards had an illustrious career with Somerset, guiding them to several one-day titles, scoring over 14,000 runs and making a career best 322 against Warwickshire in 1985. He played in 121 Tests, 187 one-day internationals and led the West Indies from 1986 until 1991. In 1988/89 he became the first Caribbean batsman to score 100 hundreds in first-class cricket.

Norman Riches
RHB, RM and occasional WK, 1900-1935

Born: Cardiff, 9 June 1883
Died: Cardiff, 6 November 1975

Batting career:

M	I	NO	Runs	Av
82	138	8	4419	33.99
(136	212	28	7228	39.28)

50	100	CT/ST
28	6	39/6
(32	16	129/27)

Bowling career:

O	M	R	W	Av
21.3	1	79	0	–
(37.5	9	143	3	47.67)

5wI	10wM
–	–

Career best performances:
177* v Leicestershire, Leicester, 1921
(217* v Dorset, Blandford Forum, 1907)
(1/1 v Berkshire, Arms Park, 1902)

Norman Riches was Glamorgan's finest batsman during their Minor County days and in 1921 he led the Welsh county in their inaugural season of Championship cricket, which included being in charge as Glamorgan won their first game against Sussex at the Arms Park.

The right-handed batsman made his Glamorgan debut in 1900 as a seventeen year old and four years later the young medical student struck 183 against Monmouthshire at Swansea. An illustrious career was being forecast for the graceful young batsman, but he opted to join his father's dental practice and, as a result, Riches only played for the Welsh county when he could get the time off.

Riches's finest season was in 1911, when he hit three centuries and repaid his father's kindness in regularly releasing him by becoming the first player in Minor County history to aggregate over 1,000 runs in a season. He was regarded by the higher authorities at Lord's as the best batsman outside the first-class game and, when available, was chosen for the Minor Counties in their games against touring teams

and first-class sides. On one occasion, he also came very close to being drafted into the MCC party to tour the West Indies.

Like many top-class county batsmen, Riches owed his success to a sound technique and unflappable temperament. His contemporaries also believed that he had as magnificent a defence as the Test players of the time. He was especially prolific on the on-side and very quick to despatch an over-pitched or short ball. He was also adept at working the ball into gaps in the field and greatly enjoyed stealing quick singles by deft placement and skilful timing of the ball.

As a youngster, Riches was an energetic cover fielder and was a safe catcher close to the wicket. Later in his career, he took to wicketkeeping and his glovework showed the same sense of purpose and resolve as his batting. Indeed, the veteran frequently went behind the stumps in 1921 when Glamorgan entered the County Championship.

It was also in 1921 that Riches became Glamorgan's first batsman to pass 1,000 runs

Left: *Norman Riches, one of the grand old men of Glamorgan CCC.* Right: *A* Western Mail *cartoon from before the Great War, showing Norman Riches's correct defence and immaculate straight bat.*

in first-class cricket and he proved his undoubted class against all of the county attacks.

However, Riches's commitments from 1922 onwards prevented him from playing in more than a dozen games in a year, and as Glamorgan suffered a series of heavy defeats, a few of the club's detractors rather scurrilously suggested that Riches was picking his games. The stalwart batsman proved these critics wrong in 1928 when, aged forty-five, he hit a masterful 140 against a powerful Lancashire attack and showed his undoubted class. This was one of nine centuries that Riches recorded in first-class cricket and he played his final Championship match in 1934 aged fifty-one. Riches retired from club cricket for Cardiff CC after the Second World War and he later became a trustee and a patron of Glamorgan CCC.

His son, John Riches, played one match for Glamorgan in 1947 and was a stalwart member of both the county's second eleven and Cardiff CC.

Norman Riches walks out to bat at the Arms Park in 1921.

Frank Ryan
LHB and SLA, 1922-1931

Born: New Jersey, 14 November 1888
Died: Leicester, 5 January 1954

Batting career:

M	I	NO	Runs	Av
215	312	100	1699	8.01

50	100	CT/ST
–	–	78

Bowling career

O	M	R	W	Av
6589.2	1317	19053	913	20.86

5wI	10wM
79	17

Career best performances:
46 v Northamptonshire, Northampton, 1925
8/41 v Derbyshire, Arms Park, 1925

Frank Ryan was perhaps one of the most colourful and charismatic characters ever to walk onto a cricket field. In the modern age his exploits off the field and little antics on it would surely have filled inch after inch of tabloid space.

Frank Ryan was educated at Bedford Grammar School and served with the Royal Flying Corps during the Great War. In 1919 he joined Hampshire as a left-arm spinner, but after two years in county cricket, punctuated by stories of a ready temper and drinking excesses, Ryan went into the Lancashire Leagues.

During 1921 the Glamorgan officials sought to strengthen their spin attack and, after consulting with Hampshire, they approached Ryan. The Glamorgan committee decided to offer terms to the maverick spinner and the story goes that a penniless Ryan hitch-hiked his way from Lancashire to Cardiff to make his Glamorgan debut in 1922.

Perhaps wary of not losing another county contract, Ryan initially showed more self-discipline and played a further 214 times until 1931, taking over 900 wickets with a high

flowing action, including career best figures of 8/41 against Derbyshire at the Arms Park in 1925. This was his finest season as he claimed 133 victims, followed by 106 in 1926.

But there were still many times when his heavy drinking and socialising affected his play and annoyed the Glamorgan hierarchy. During one away match, he was found fast asleep under the covers, having forgotten where the team were staying. On another occasion after play against Lancashire, he carried on drinking with his friends until the early hours of the morning, before travelling by taxi from Manchester to Cardiff to rejoin the rest of the side. He apparently entered the Glamorgan dressing room saying, 'Ryan never lets you down', and handed over the taxi bill to the county's treasurer.

Had it not been for these excesses, many believe that Ryan could have won a Test cap, but at the end of the 1931 season he was released by the Glamorgan officials who said farewell to several professionals as an economy measure. He returned to league cricket in Lancashire and Yorkshire after an eventful career.

Born: Bombay, 27 May 1962

Batting career:

M	I	NO	Runs	Av
62	98	18	3402	42.53
74	*72*	*14*	*1985*	*34.22*

50	100	CT/ST
20	6	32
13	*1*	*21*

Bowling career:

O	M	R	W	Av
1307.4	340	3228	95	33.98
475.1	*25*	*1914*	*51*	*37.53*

5wI	10wM
3	–

Career best performances:
157 v Somerset, Sophia Gardens, 1988
7/49 v Lancashire, Swansea, 1988
138 v Minor Counties, Trowbridge, 1991*
5/13 v Scotland, Edinburgh, 1988

Ravi Shastri was the first (and so far only) Indian Test cricketer to play for Glamorgan, and his aggressive, yet elegant, batting and steady left-arm spin were important elements in Glamorgan's success in the one-day form of county cricket during the late 1980s and early 1990s.

Shastri made his first-class debut as a seventeen year old in Indian domestic cricket in 1979 and in 1980/81 he made his Test debut against England. He subsequently appeared in 43 Tests and 150 one-day internationals, besides being Player of the Tournament in the 1984/85 World Championship of Cricket in Australia.

Shastri also holds the world record for the fastest ever double century in first-class cricket, having hit 200* off just 123 balls in only 113 minutes for Bombay against Baroda in the Ranji Trophy at Bombay. During this career best performance, Shastri hit 13 sixes, including six in an over from Tilak Raj.

The Indian joined Glamorgan in 1987 and made an immediate impact with both bat and ball in the limited-over games. His accurate left-arm spin and explosive batting helped the club to a semi-final place in 1988 in the Benson & Hedges Cup, as well as a series of Sunday League victories.

He also struck 6 first-class centuries for the Welsh county, including 157 against Somerset at Sophia Gardens in 1988, 127 and 101* in the match against Middlesex at Abergavenny in 1989 and 133* against Lancashire at Liverpool in 1991. Each contained a series of well-timed boundaries and crisply-struck drives.

Shastri also took over 140 wickets in all forms of cricket for the Welsh county, despite temporarily losing his action. He retired from first-class cricket in 1994 and is now a well-known cricket commentator and presenter on television and radio.

Don Shepherd
RHB and RFM or OB, 1950-1972

Born: Port Eynon, 12 August 1927

Batting career:

M	I	NO	Runs	Av
647	816	241	5610	9.75
73	*43*	*20*	*190*	*8.26*

50	100	CT/ST
5	–	241
–	–	*18*

Bowling career:

O	M	R	W	Av
21514.2	7334	45571	2174	20.95
579.1	*94*	*1937*	*99*	*19.57*

5wI	10wM
122	28

Career best performances:
73 v Derbyshire, Arms Park, 1961
9/47 v Northants, Arms Park, 1954
25* v Leicestershire, Coalville, 1970
5/31 v Northants, Northampton, 1969

Don Shepherd took more wickets than any other bowler who has not played Test cricket. The off-cutter's record of 2,174 wickets for Glamorgan in first-class cricket, at just over 20 apiece, speaks volumes for Shepherd's ability and perseverance over a career with the Welsh county from 1950 until 1972. It also highlights the way English cricket in the 1950s and 1960s was well blessed with spinners such as Jim Laker, Fred Titmus and Derek Underwood, for Shepherd to be constantly overlooked at the highest level.

Shepherd made his Glamorgan debut in 1950 against Surrey at The Oval as a seam bowler and until 1955 he was a fast-medium bowler. In these early years, he regularly opened the bowling and in 1952 he claimed 115 victims and won his county cap after taking 11/101 against Lancashire at Preston. However, he lost form and penetration during 1955 and he found it difficult to regularly hit the seam. He sought advice from Wilf Wooller and other senior players, and decided to convert to off-cutters. After hours of practice, he took 10/85 against Warwickshire at Neath in the final match of the season, and 'Shep' decided to concentrate on off-spin in 1956.

His change of style reaped handsome rewards in 1956, as Shepherd took 168 wickets for the county, taking more than 5 wickets in an innings on 15 occasions. He passed the 100 mark in 11 further seasons and Shepherd tricked and teased the finest batsmen on the county circuit for years. He was fortunate to have the support of some top-class close fielders, especially Peter Walker and wicketkeepers Haydn Davies, David Evans and Eifion Jones, who were instructed by 'Shep' to stand back rather than up to the stumps. This was not surprising as Shepherd was not a classical slow bowler: he delivered the ball at almost medium pace and had the ability to undercut the ball and make it move in the air, thereby causing the batsman to misjudge the length of the ball.

He was a match-winner on a turning wicket, as testified by a series of remarkable returns, including 6/5 against Nottinghamshire at Newport in 1961, 5/2 against Leicestershire at Ebbw Vale in 1965 and 7/7 against Hampshire at the Arms Park in 1966, whilst he took a hat-trick

Don Shepherd receives the Man of the Match award from Charles Barnett after hitting a six to win Glamorgan's Gillette Cup match against Worcestershire at Newport in 1964

against Northamptonshire at Swansea in 1964. He was also an aggressive lower-order batsman who equalled the world record with a whirlwind half-century against the 1961 Australians at Swansea, reaching 50 in just 15 minutes. He recorded only 11 scoring strokes, hitting 6 sixes, 3 fours, a two and a single.

Shepherd was also a canny tactician, acting as a wise senior professional from 1962, and he was Tony Lewis's loyal vice-captain during the Championship winning season in 1969. The year before, 'Shep' had led Glamorgan to victory over the 1968 Australians at Swansea, and the 79-run victory was a tribute to his subtle tactics and shrewd bowling changes. He adapted well to the new demands of Sunday League cricket, recording figures of 5/31 at Northampton in Glamorgan's first match in the new forty-over Sunday competition on 27 April 1969.

In 1969/70 Shepherd toured Ceylon and the Far East with the MCC, and in 1970 he was a *Wisden* Cricketer of the Year. He retired in 1972, but has kept close to the county game by coaching and working on BBC Radio Wales.

The fine bowling action of Don Shepherd during one of Glamorgan's Championship matches in 1968.

Cyril Smart
RHB and LB, 1927-1946

Born: Lacock, Wiltshire, 23 July 1898
Died: Abertillery, 21 May 1975

Batting career:

M	I	NO	Runs	Av
190	301	35	8069	30.34

50	100	CT/ST
46	9	123

Bowling career:

O	M	R	W	Av
2097.4	302	6943	169	41.08

5wI	10wM
1	–

Career best performances:
151* v Sussex, Hastings, 1935
5/39 v Somerset, Weston-Super-Mare, 1939

Cyril Smart was one of the most explosive batsmen in county cricket before the Second World War and in 1935 he created a world record by hitting Hampshire's Gerry Hill for 32 in an over at the Arms Park. Smart struck 6, 6, 4, 6, 6 and 4, each from authentic strokes, cleanly hit in an arc from straight to deep square leg, and his second four was just inches short of crossing the boundary for a fifth six.

Earlier in the 1935 season, Smart had also made 114* against the South Africans, and he shared a partnership of 131 with debutant Wilf Hughes – which created a club record for the tenth wicket and saved Glamorgan from defeat. Smart celebrated his hundred by lofting a ball out of the Arms Park and straight through the plate glass window in the foyer of a hotel in the adjoining Westgate Street. In all games in 1935, Smart hit 30 sixes – a club record – including 6 in his career best score of 151* against Sussex at Hastings, with one of his blows going high over the seating area, out of the ground, and into the back garden of a house.

Smart had initially played for Warwickshire from 1920 until 1922, before joining Briton Ferry Town as their professional and qualifying for Glamorgan. He made his debut for the Welsh county in 1927, but he did not win a regular place until 1934. It was not long though before his big hitting made him very popular with their supporters and he passed 1,000 runs every summer bar one from 1934 until 1939.

Smart was a strongly built man, with a rather hunched stance, but this did not affect his run-scoring. According to J.C. Clay, 'he was probably the best number six in England, and was not by any means a hitter pure and simple. His defensive play was correctness itself, with a bat as straight as a plumb line.'

He also played in every one of Glamorgan's wartime friendlies, often at great inconvenience to himself, but he was keen to support the club that had shown so much faith in him. When the Championship resumed in 1946, he helped out Glamorgan for one final season, before retiring and becoming a publican in Abertillery.

Billy Spiller
RHB, 1905-1923

Born: St Fagan's, 8 July 1886
Died: Cardiff, 9 June 1970

Batting career:

M	I	NO	Runs	Av
13	22	0	411	18.68
(4	6	1	46	9.20)

50	100	CT/ST
1	1	7
(–	–	1)

Bowling career:

O	M	R	W	Av
4.0	0	31	0	–

5wI	10wM
–	–

Career best performances:
104 v Northamptonshire, Northampton, 1921
(24* Surrey 2nd XI, The Oval, 1905)

Billy Spiller created a unique place for himself in the annals of Glamorgan CCC by recording their first ever hundred in the County Championship. What was even more remarkable was that before 1921 he had last played for Glamorgan back in 1908.

Spiller had played both cricket and rugby for Cardiff in the early 1900s, and he won 10 Welsh rugby caps between 1909 and 1912, playing as a centre against Scotland, Ireland, England, France and South Africa. He made his Glamorgan debut in Minor County matches during 1905, but the right-handed batsman was unable to play for the county after 1908 owing to his duties with the South Wales Constabulary.

He continued to play in club cricket for St Fagan's, Cardiff and Barry, and was considered by many to be the best Welsh-born batsman. The promotion of Glamorgan into the County Championship in 1921 was good news for Spiller, as he was able to gain leave during July and August to play in the county side. Despite his long absence from the county side, he showed that he had not lost any of his stroke-making talents and on 26 July 1921 he made Glamorgan's first-ever Championship century with an innings of 104 during the game with Northamptonshire at Northampton.

He was only able to play on two further occasions – against Yorkshire at Headingley in 1922, and again in 1923 against Gloucestershire at Cheltenham. Had he been able to get more time off from his police duties, Spiller would surely have become a heavy scorer for Glamorgan, recording more than just a single hundred. Later in life he took up bowls and also represented the county at this game. He eventually retired from the Glamorgan police force at the rank of inspector.

Jimmy Stone
RHB and WK, 1922-1923

Born: Southampton, 29 November 1876
Died: Maidenhead, 15 November 1942

Batting career:

M	I	NO	Runs	Av
27	48	2	1047	22.76

50	100	CT/ST
5	1	26/12

Career best performance:
108 v West Indians, Arms Park, 1923

Jimmy Stone has a special place in Glamorgan's record books as he recorded their first ever century against a touring team. The wicketkeeper reached this landmark with 108 against the 1923 West Indians at Cardiff Arms Park – and at the age of forty-six! His innings occurred during a partnership of 136 in an hour and a half with Frank Pinch, and their stand laid the foundation for a 43-run victory for the Glamorgan side.

Stone had previously played for Hampshire, making his debut in 1900. One of his finest hours with his native county came in 1912 when his nimble work behind the stumps was a feature of Hampshire's victory over the Australians by 8 wickets. In all, he spent fifteen years on the Hampshire staff, during which time he passed 1,000 runs on 3 occasions, and developed into a capable and unobtrusive wicketkeeper. During this time, he claimed over 300 dismissals in 274 first-class appearances until 1914.

After the Great War, he moved to South Wales and joined Briton Ferry Town, where he qualified by residence for Glamorgan. The Welshmen had lacked the services of a regular wicketkeeper in their inaugural season and had used a variety of amateurs and occasional 'keepers. They were very grateful to have the services of the Hampshire veteran, who made his debut in 1922 against Northamptonshire at Swansea. He was a regular behind the stumps in 1923, but this proved to be his only full season with the Welsh county, as he decided to retire from playing in 1924, and became an umpire, standing in first-class cricket from 1925 until 1934.

In all first-class cricket, Stone made 10,341 runs with a career best score of 174 for Hampshire. He also took 394 catches and made 130 stumpings.

Jock Tait

RHB and OB, 1911-1926

Born: Shetland Islands, 20 November 1886
Died: Bristol, 13 April 1945
Batting career:

M	I	NO	Runs	Av
43	81	1	1475	18.43
(30	49	4	1195	26.56)

50	100	CT/ST
7	–	20
(7	–	11)

Bowling career:

O	M	R	W	Av
21.0	4	87	1	87.00
(36.0	6	134	3	44.67)

5wI	10wM
–	–

Career best performances:
96 v Sussex, Arms Park, 1921
1/5 v Sussex, Hove, 1922
(93 v Durham, Sunderland, 1914)
(1/17 v Surrey 2nd XI, The Oval, 1920)

'Jock' Tait very nearly wrote himself a place in Glamorgan's history by scoring 96 against Sussex in the county's inaugural first-class match in 1921, thereby coming within four runs of becoming the club's first Championship centurion, and he would have achieved this feat on his first-class debut.

Born in the Shetland Islands in November 1886, Tait was a multi-talented sportsman, as he displayed on moving to work in South Wales in the early 1900s. He played cricket and rugby for Swansea, football for Cardiff Corinthians and Newport County, and won a Welsh Amateur Football cap in 1913, playing against England at Llandudno.

Tait made his Glamorgan debut in Minor County cricket in 1911 and the right-handed batsman confirmed his promise by hitting 100* in the friendly against Sir Henry Webb's XI at Cardiff Arms Park in 1913. In 1914 he made 93 against Durham at Sunderland and just seemed to be fulfilling his potential when the Great War broke out, depriving Tait of further opportunities to produce big innings for the county. He served as a lieutenant in the Welch Regiment during the war, but he had to be taken home with a leg injury and shrapnel wounds, which resulted in his retirement from rugby and football.

Fortunately, he was still able to play cricket and when club cricket resumed in 1919, Tait continued to be a heavy scorer for Cardiff and the amateur was regularly chosen in the county side when Glamorgan were elevated to the County Championship in 1921. He had a thriving insurance business in the docks at Cardiff and Swansea, and with a host of useful contacts, he agreed to serve on the county's committee from 1921 until 1926.

In 1923 Tait led the county side in several games when regular captain Tom Whittington was unavailable and he also appeared several times for Wales, before retiring from the county game in 1926.

Greg Thomas
RHB and RF, 1979-1988

Born: Trebannos, 12 August 1960

Batting career:

M	I	NO	Runs	Av
106	139	24	2137	18.58
104	*90*	*19*	*895*	*12.60*

50	100	CT/ST
4	2	38
–	–	*19*

Bowling career:

O	M	R	W	Av
2239.5	386	8230	256	32.25
745.0	*65*	*3319*	*121*	*27.43*

5wI	10wM
9	1

Career best performances:
110 v Warwickshire, Edgbaston, 1988
6/68 v Nottinghamshire, Sophia Gardens, 1988
37 v Nottinghamshire, Trent Bridge, 1985
5/17 Sussex, Sophia Gardens, 1985

Greg Thomas was the first fluent Welsh speaker to play Test cricket and the man who earned the tag of 'the fastest white man' in English cricket in the mid-1980s after some fiery spells for Glamorgan and Border. His pace and hostility won him a place on England's tour to the Caribbean in 1985/86, and in the First Test he nearly took a wicket with his first two deliveries in Test cricket, as Desmond Haynes edged his first ball over the head of first slip, before being dropped in the gully off Thomas's second delivery.

This was the first of 5 Tests and 3 one-day internationals that Thomas appeared in during a ten-year career with Glamorgan that had begun with making his debut against the Sri Lankans at Swansea in 1979. However, he was not a regular in the county side until 1984, by which time he had completed his college studies and had undergone surgery for a stress fracture in his back.

Despite his selection for England, various ailments and injuries dogged Thomas's career with Glamorgan and he failed to take 50 Championship wickets during any of his seasons with the county. His most productive summer was in 1988 when he claimed 48 first-class wickets at an average of 31. There was no doubting that Thomas could deliver the ball at blistering pace, but he was also erratic at times, and became frustrated by the slow Welsh wickets which he felt were hindering his claims of gaining Test recognition.

In 1989 Thomas joined Northamptonshire and in 1989/90 he went on Mike Gatting's 'rebel' England tour to South Africa. In 1990 he took a career best 7/75, ironically for Northamptonshire against his former employers, but he lost his place with the English county the following year after sustaining a pelvic injury, and was forced to retire at the end of the 1991 season.

Darren Thomas
LHB and RFM, 1992-present

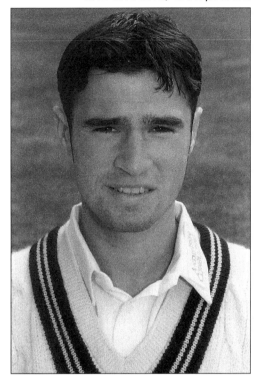

Born: Morriston, 25 January 1975

Batting career:

M	I	NO	Runs	Av
89	121	25	1788	18.63
68	*52*	*10*	*568*	*13.52*

50	100	CT/ST
8	–	36
–	–	*13*

Bowling career:

O	M	R	W	Av
2340.5	365	8481	279	30.40
455.0	*17*	*2338*	*93*	*25.14*

5wI	10wM
12	–

Career best performances:
78* v Gloucestershire, Abergavenny, 1995
5/24 v Sussex, Swansea, 1997
40 v Hants Board XI, Southampton, 1998
7/16 v Surrey, Swansea, 1998

In 1998 Darren Thomas recorded the best-ever analysis for Glamorgan in one-day cricket, by taking 7/16 in the AXA League match against Surrey at Swansea. He had previously hit the headlines on his county debut in 1992 when he took 5/80 against Derbyshire at Chesterfield aged 17 years and 212 days. The young Llanelli pace bowler subsequently won a place in the Young England side and started to show rich promise with the bat, as testified by a career best 78* against Gloucestershire at Abergavenny in 1995.

Despite being erratic at times, there was no denying that Thomas could bowl with genuine pace and hostility, as testified by a return of 6/20 against the Combined Universities at Cardiff in 1995. He rather lost his way in 1996, but under the wise guidance of coach Duncan Fletcher he made rapid headway during 1997. His greater accuracy and strike rate were two of the chief factors behind Glamorgan's Championship quest, and it was fitting that Thomas should bowl Glamorgan to victory at Taunton and to the Championship title in 1997.

Thomas consolidated on his achievements with a marvellous season in 1998, finishing the summer as the county's leading wicket-taker with 71 first-class victims at 24 apiece. He was rewarded with a place in the England 'A' party for the 1998/99 tour to South Africa and Zimbabwe, although some people felt that in comparison with some of the players chosen in the full England party for Australia, Thomas could have gained selection for the Ashes tour. He responded with 8 wickets in the first 'Test' and then, in the 1999 season for Glamorgan, he ended up as the county's leading wicket-taker once again. Despite his success, he was not initially chosen for the 'A' tour to Bangladesh and New Zealand in 1999/2000, but following Chris Silverwood's promotion to the full England tour, Thomas was called out to New Zealand, where once again he impressed with his pace and hostility.

Stan Trick

RHB and LM or SLA, 1946-1950

Born: Briton Ferry, 31 October 1916
Died: Morriston, 27 October 1995

Batting career:

M	I	NO	Runs	Av
19	22	11	52	4.72

50	100	CT/ST
–	–	9

Bowling career:

O	M	R	W	Av
515.3	196	1087	56	19.41

5wI	10wM
4	2

Career best performances:
15 v Leicestershire, Swansea, 1949
6/29 v Somerset, Swansea, 1948

Stan Trick was a prolific wicket-taker for Neath and Briton Ferry Steel in the South Wales Cricket Association either side of the Second World War and, on his few appearances at first-class level between 1946 and 1950, he proved to be a match-winning spin bowler.

As a schoolboy in the 1930s, Trick showed great prowess as a cricketer and a footballer. He won international football honours for Welsh Schoolboys and even agreed terms with Brentwood, but he never turned professional and opted to stay in the Neath area, where he could work at his family's motor garage and play cricket in the South Wales leagues.

His prodigious wicket-taking feats with left-arm spin for Neath brought him to the attention of the county selectors and he made his Second XI debut in Minor County games in 1936. Despite some impressive performances, his work commitments prevented him from playing on a full-time basis and it wasn't until 1946 that he made his first-class debut.

Despite only appearing infrequently, Trick proved to be wily bowler and he was particularly useful on the dry, turning wickets at Swansea. Indeed, it was at the St Helen's ground in 1948 where Trick produced both a career best and match-winning performance against Somerset, when he claimed six wickets in each innings with his clever spin and subtle flight. He impressed many good judges during these occasional appearances and according to Fred Root, the former Worcestershire and England bowler, Trick had the ability to play for England and could have filled the gap after the war caused by the death of Hedley Verity.

Standing at over six feet tall, Trick used his height to gain sharp turn from the pitch. On damper and greener surfaces, he judiciously mixed up his left-arm spin with little swingers – both in and out – often keeping batsmen guessing as to the nature of the next delivery.

During the Second World War, Trick held a commission in the Army and played with considerable success in service matches, confirming that had he not been so heavily involved with his family's business, Trick could have progressed onto higher honours.

Born: Cardiff, 16 March 1906
Died: Montchamp, France, 5 August 1944

Batting career:

M	I	NO	Runs	Av
314	504	25	14431	30.12

50	100	CT/ST
74	22	253

Bowling career:

O	M	R	W	Av
46.4	2	266	2	133.00

5wI	10wM
–	–

Career best performances:
233 v Worcestershire, Swansea, 1937
1/4 v Somerset, Bath, 1931

Maurice Turnbull, one of the club's finest ever batsmen, most inspirational captains and their first ever Test cricketer, was killed in action in August 1944 whilst on active service in France. His single-minded efforts during the 1930s transformed a team of habitual losers with large debts to a successful outfit with financial reserves. Throughout his career, Turnbull's name had been closely associated with affairs of the county club and who knows what else this great figure would have achieved had he not been killed during the Second World War.

Turnbull was a member of a prominent ship-owning family from Penarth and he went to school at Downside School in Somerset, where he established a series of batting records. He made his county debut in 1924 whilst still at school and ended up as Glamorgan's top scorer in the match with Lancashire at Swansea.

In 1926 Turnbull went to Trinity College, Cambridge, where he won three cricket Blues and led the university XI in 1929. During the summer, he scored over 1,000 runs for Cambridge and, after leaving university, he continued to be Glamorgan's most prolific batsman. It had been clear for many years that Turnbull was destined for higher honours and at the end of the 1929 season he duly won selection for the MCC tour of Australia and New Zealand. In January 1930 he made his Test debut at Christchurch and thereby became the first Glamorgan player to win an England Test cap.

On his return to Britain, Turnbull took over the captaincy of Glamorgan and over the next decade he transformed the downtrodden county into a successful playing unit. He was a gifted leader, always getting the best out of the motley assortment of amateurs and hard-nosed professionals who were at his disposal. He also put great faith in the young Welsh players and helped to create a clear Welsh identity in Glamorgan CCC, thereby raising public interest in South Wales and boosting gate receipts.

He was also very active off the field and in 1932 took over the duties of the club's secretary. Together with his close friend Johnnie Clay, they used their business and social contacts to raise cash for the poverty-stricken club through a

Left: *Maurice Turnbull while he was an undergraduate at Cambridge.* Right: *A sketch of Maurice Turnbull from the* Piccadilly *magazine, showing his classical cover drive.*

special fund-raising appeal. Their actions ensured the club avoided bankrupcy. It was claimed that during the winter of 1932/33 Turnbull danced more miles than he had scored runs the previous summer – an impressive feat considering that he had passed the 1,300 run mark!

In 1933 Turnbull made 200* against Northamptonshire and he was recalled to the England side at Lord's and The Oval. He also led the Rest in the Test trial in 1934 and, as he had at Glamorgan, revealed an astute cricket brain. Indeed, Turnbull has been described as the best of his generation never to captain England. He was certainly worth his place as a batsman, but he rather fell out with the MCC authorities over what they viewed as 'illegal' declarations. In fact, all that Turnbull was trying to do was to provide entertaining cricket in rain-affected games. His actions would not have been censured in the modern era, but Turnbull was severely reprimanded by the authorities.

Turnbull's Test career was restricted to 9 matches, but Glamorgan benefited by having his undivided attention. In fact, after his spat with the MCC, it was clear that Turnbull preferred his county duties, as in 1933/34 he turned down an invitation to tour India and devoted his winter to further fund-raising for Glamorgan. However, Turnbull was back in favour at Lord's in 1938 when he was appointed an England selector.

Turnbull was also an outstanding rugby player, playing as a half-back for Cardiff and winning 2 Welsh caps in 1932. He was also a Welsh hockey international in 1929 and played with distinction for the Cardiff club, besides winning a hockey Blue whilst at Cambridge. During his career, Turnbull amassed 17,544 runs, and hit 29 centuries, including a career best 233 against Worcestershire at Swansea. There is no knowing how many more runs he would have scored or what other feats Maurice Turnbull would have achieved had he not given his life for his country whilst serving with the Welsh Guards during the Normandy Invasion.

Born: Clifton, 17 February 1936

Batting career:

M	I	NO	Runs	Av
437	738	106	16510	26.12
72	*68*	*7*	*1218*	*19.97*

50	100	CT/ST
86	12	656
4	*–*	*32*

Bowling career:

O	M	R	W	Av
8879.0	2749	21652	771	28.08
306.4	*40*	*1065*	*52*	*20.48*

5wI	10wM
22	2

Career best performances:
152* v Middlesex, Lord's, 1962
7/58 v Middesex, Lord's, 1962
79 v Staffordshire, Stoke, 1971
5/21 v Cornwall, Truro, 1970

In the eyes of many people, Peter Walker was the finest close catcher in post-war county cricket. He fully utilised his tall frame when standing fearlessly at short-leg, or in the slips, and he held many stunning catches in the days when fielders only wore a box for protection, unlike the modern era of helmets and shin-pads.

During his career with Glamorgan from 1956 until 1972, Walker set a host of fielding records which still stand today, including 8 catches in the match with Derbyshire at Swansea in 1970, 67 catches in 1961 and a career tally of 656 victims.

Walker was born in Clifton, Bristol, and grew up in South Africa, before spending a couple of years in the Merchant Navy, where he developed his catching skills throwing potatoes around the deck! When he was a schoolboy in Johannesburg, Walker was coached by Allan Watkins, so when he visited his grandparents in South Wales in 1952, Walker decided to contact his old coach. A trial with Glamorgan soon followed

and he joined the full-time staff in 1955 as an attacking middle-order batsman and a left-arm swing bowler.

In 1956 he made his first-class debut against Yorkshire at Swansea and his lively swing bowling won him a regular place. He also developed a slower style, after experimenting with the old ball, and his left-arm spin complemented the off-breaks of McConnon and Shepherd. In 1959 Walker passed the 1,500 run mark, hitting just a single century, but proving his consistency with 14 fifties.

In 1960 the England selectors recognised his potential by including him in their side for the first three Tests against South Africa. By his own admission, he was in modest form with the bat when he won his first Test cap, but he owed his call-up to a vacancy in the England middle-order, and a useful all-round performance for the MCC against the Springboks at Lord's. According to *Wisden* he marked his Test debut at Edgbaston with 'some powerful off-drives and sweeps', and in

Peter Walker turns the ball to leg during Glamorgan's match against Leicestershire at Grace Road in 1971.

the three matches he played his part efficiently without ever dominating proceedings. Even so, his efforts saw England record comfortable victories in all three Tests, but he was subsequently omitted as the selectors experimented with other choices.

Although he never got another chance at Test level, Walker remained an integral member of the Glamorgan side of the 1960s. His most productive season was in 1962 when he scored over 1,500 runs, with centuries against Yorkshire and Middlesex, and took 89 first-class wickets. In 1965 and 1966 he scored over 1,000 runs once again, both times without hitting a century, and he claimed over 50 wickets in 1967, 1969 and 1970. He also became a very useful performer in limited-overs cricket, taking

4/21 against Warwickshire in their 1970 Sunday League match at Edgbaston, as well as 5/21 against Cornwall at Truro in the 1970 Gillette Cup.

Walker retired at the end of the 1972 season and subsequently became a leading broadcaster and journalist. He also acted as chief executive of the Cricket Board of Wales, overseeing the introduction of a nation-wide coaching framework across Wales and the development of the National Cricket Centre at Glamorgan's headquarters at Sophia Gardens. Yet all of this might never have happened had Walker not hitch-hiked several thousand miles to see his Welsh grandfather and then walked into Glamorgan's offices in High Street, Cardiff, to ask for a job in cricket!

Born: Bedlinog, 28 August 1905
Died: Neath, 23 December 1992

Batting career:

M	I	NO	Runs	Av
75	133	9	2146	17.31

50	100	CT/ST
5	2	23
–	–	–

Bowling career:

O	M	R	W	Av
5.2	0	37	0	–

5wI	10wM
–	–

Career best performance:
116 v Warwickshire, Swansea, 1926

Cyril Walters was one of the bright young hopes of Glamorgan cricket during the 1920s and in 1934 he captained England against Australia at Trent Bridge when Bob Wyatt fractured his thumb. By this time, however, Walters was a Worcestershire player after he joined them in 1928 as their player-secretary.

Educated at Neath Grammar School, Walters made his Glamorgan debut in 1923 as a seventeen year old against Lancashire. He appeared regularly in 1924 and 1925, but only managed a half-century against Worcestershire at New Road in 1924. However, there was no doubting his potential, nor his youthful flair in the field – which contrasted with the heavy girth and greying hair of several of his colleagues – so, despite a lack of runs, his presence was greatly appreciated by these portly amateurs.

The elegant young batsman seemed to have turned the corner in 1926, when he struck two centuries at Swansea, against Warwickshire and Leicestershire, and fifties against Somerset and Yorkshire. He showed a wide range of elegant, flowing strokes, and developed into a good accumulator off his legs, with a powerful and classical off-drive. However, Walters had several business interests and in 1927 he only appeared in the opening six games, before concentrating on his career as an architect and surveyor. He reappeared briefly in 1928, but then announced that he was joining Worcestershire, making his debut for them later that season against the West Indies. The loss of the gifted young amateur was not fully appreciated until the 1930s, when Walters hit a career best score of 226 for Worcestershire against Kent at Gravesend in 1933. This was his most successful season, during which he set a new county record of 9 centuries.

By this time, he had won the first of 11 Test caps and he went on to open the batting for England and was a member of the MCC touring party to India and Ceylon in 1933/34. Unlike many other batsmen, Walters easily bridged the gap between county and Test cricket, as confirmed by a Test average of 52.26 compared with his overall first-class average of just 30.74. Ill health and domestic commitments forced Walters into retirement in 1935.

Waqar Younis
RHB and RF, 1997-1998

Born: Vehari, Pakistan, 16 November 1969

Batting career:

M	I	NO	Runs	Av
20	23	1	328	14.91
22	*12*	*4*	*182*	*22.75*

50	100	CT/ST
–	–	4
–	*–*	*2*

Bowling career:

O	M	R	W	Av
541.5	96	1948	80	24.35
168.3	*12*	*796*	*33*	*24.12*

5wI	10wM
3	1

Career best performances:
47 v Kent, Canterbury, 1998
8/17 v Sussex, Swansea, 1997
45 v Sussex, Hove, 1998
4/14 v Sussex, Swansea, 1997

Waqar Younis was Glamorgan's overseas player when they won the Championship in 1997. During that summer the Pakistani spearheaded the Welsh attack, claiming 68 wickets at 22. In a remarkable week in June, Waqar took 7/25, including a hat-trick, as Lancashire were dismissed at Liverpool for just 51, before returning match figures of 8/34 at Swansea as Sussex were bowled out for 54 and 67. These amazing spells of top-class fast bowling produced two comprehensive victories for Glamorgan (by 221 and 234 runs respectively) and helped to set them on the way to the Championship title.

He also played a key role in 1997 as Glamorgan reached the semi-finals of the NatWest Trophy. In the match at Southampton against Hampshire, he shared a ninth-wicket partnership with Adrian Shaw which saw Glamorgan home by two wickets with just two balls to spare. Then, in the quarter-final at Cardiff, Waqar hit an unbeaten 34 against Yorkshire and shared an unbroken partnership of 28 with last man Dean Cosker to see Glamorgan home by one wicket in nail-biting conditions.

Sadly, he struggled with injury the following season and left Glamorgan at the end of 1998 with a total of 113 first-class wickets from 42 appearances. The Pakistani had previously played for Surrey between 1990 and 1993, taking 232 wickets in three seasons of Championship cricket, including 113 in 1991 at just 14 apiece.

In the early 1990s, Waqar was one of the most feared bowlers in county and international cricket, producing devastating spells of new ball bowling, as well as getting prodigious reverse swing with the old ball. Often he finished off an innings with a series of fast, in-swinging yorkers that proved far too good for tail-enders.

After an innocuous performance on his debut against India in 1989, Waqar burst onto the international scene in 1990, with some fine returns on the lifeless Sharjah wicket. His career was interrupted by a back problem, which caused him to miss the 1992 World Cup and most of the 1995 cricketing year. Despite this, Waqar jointly holds the record for reaching 200 wickets in the least number of Tests. He has played in 58 Tests and over 180 one-day internationals.

Steve Watkin

RHB and RFM, 1986-present

Born: Maesteg, 15 September 1964

Batting career:

M	I	NO	Runs	Av
222	250	94	1645	10.54
215	*96*	*38*	*404*	*6.97*

50	100	CT/ST
–	–	61
–	*–*	*34*

Bowling career:

O	M	R	W	Av
7351.4	1707	21335	770	27.71
1770.4	*202*	*7010*	*268*	*26.16*

5wI	10wM
28	4

Career best performances:
41 v Worcestershire, Worcester, 1992
8/59 v Warwickshire, Edgbaston, 1988
31* v Derbyshire, Checkley, 1991
5/23 v Warwickshire, Edgbaston, 1990

Day in, day out Steve Watkin has been one of the most reliable bowlers on the county circuit. The cheerful seamer has shouldered the burden of being both strike and stock bowler in the Glamorgan attack for almost every year since winning a regular place in the side in 1988. Despite a workload that might frighten other English bowlers, Watkin has never had a serious injury, and his consistency was rewarded with nomination as one of *Wisden's* Cricketers of the Year in 1993. Given his consistency and wholehearted efforts, many people, inside and out of Wales, feel that Watkin should have played more for England.

Watkin first made his mark for Glamorgan in the second half of 1988 when he took 46 wickets and recorded career best figures of 8/59 against Warwickshire at Edgbaston. In 1989 he took a further 92 wickets and won both his county cap and selection on the England 'A' tour in 1989/90 to East Africa and Zimbabwe.

In 1990 Watkin took 65 wickets and in the next 7 seasons he claimed over 50 first-class wickets. His consistency was rewarded with a place on the England 'A' tour to Pakistan and Sri Lanka, and in 1991 he made his Test debut against the West Indies at Headingley. The Glamorgan seamer rose to the occasion, taking 3/38 in the tourists' second innings as England won by 115 runs. Watkin reappeared in the Second Test of the series at Lord's, although he failed to take any wickets, and was omitted for the rest of the series. However, he remained in the selectors' thoughts and toured the West Indies with England 'A' in 1991/92.

After his winter in the Caribbean, Watkin claimed 86 wickets during 1993 and regained his place in the England side for the Sixth Test of the Ashes series at The Oval. Matthew Maynard was also in the England side, making this Test the first time two Glamorgan players had been chosen by England. It proved to be a successful one, both for the Welsh and English contingents, with Watkin taking 4/65 in Australia's

Left: *Steve Watkin bowling for Glamorgan against Warwickshire at Edgbaston in April 1990.*
Right: *Another fine delivery from Steve Watkin during his highly successful season in 1989.*

second innings and England winning by 161 runs.

Watkin's efforts at The Oval resulted in his inclusion in the England party for the 1993/94 tour of the West Indies. Although not making the Test team, Watkin did appear in four of the one-day internationals and took 4/49 in the second match of the series at Kingston. This tour was the final time that Watkin appeared in England colours and with a Test record of two wins and a draw, he can lay claim to having never been on a losing England side in Test cricket.

Despite not being chosen again for England, Watkin has continued to be a most reliable opening bowler in Championship cricket and his experience with the new ball was evident during 1997 as Glamorgan won the County Championship. He benefitted by having Waqar Younis as a new ball partner and, with Darren Thomas also making

headway, Glamorgan had a potent pace attack. During 1997 Watkin claimed 61 first-class wickets at 22 runs apiece. His fine haul included 7/41 against Leicestershire at Grace Road.

He is widely regarded by umpires and fellow professionals to have been one of the best and well-mannered new ball bowlers in English county cricket during the 1990s. It was fitting that after Glamorgan's Championship win in 1997, Steve was awarded a benefit year in 1998. It proved to be a highly successful as Steve secured a sum in excess of £130,000 to his credit. This spoke volumes for the high regard in which he is held by the club's supporters and it was a worthy reward for one of the game's most popular professionals. During Steve's career, Glamorgan have won the County Championship, the Sunday League and appeared in a Lord's final.

Allan Watkins

LHB and LM, 1939-1961

Born: Usk, 21 April 1922

Batting career:

M	I	NO	Runs	Av
407	649	76	17419	30.39

50	100	CT/ST
89	29	390

Bowling career:

O	M	R	W	Av
7497.5	2027	17683	774	22.84

5wI	10wM
24	–

Career best performances:
170* v Leicestershire, Swansea, 1954
7/28 v Derbyshire, Chesterfield, 1954

The jovial and energetic Allan Watkins was the first Glamorgan player to appear at home for England in an Ashes series, achieving this feat in 1948 by playing against Australia at The Oval. The following winter he also became the county's first centurion in Test cricket, scoring 111 in the Fourth Test against South Africa at Johannesburg. In all, Watkins won 15 caps and this still remains a club record, shared jointly with Jeff Jones and Robert Croft, for the most number of appearances for England in Test matches.

The all-rounder gave yeoman service to the Welsh county between 1939 and 1961 and, in his early years, Watkins mixed county cricket with professional football for Plymouth Argyle and Cardiff City. In fact, his maiden century was achieved at the Arms Park in 1946 only after the Argyle manager had agreed to release the winger from training.

Watkins was a solid and enterprising left-handed batsman, who could also bowl left-arm seam and cutters. His all-round skills, mix of flowing strokeplay and gritty defence, and alert fielding close to the wicket made him a popular figure with Glamorgan's supporters and a well-respected figure on the county circuit.

These qualities were also recognised by the England selectors, who appointed him as senior professional on their tour to India, Pakistan and Ceylon in 1951/52. He wholeheartedly undertook the role of stock bowler and also finished the tour as the leading run scorer in the Test series with India. His determination was also to the fore during a nine-hour vigil in the First Test at Delhi and his 137* helped to save England from defeat.

In 1954 and 1955, Watkins performed the double and in 1955/56 he served as senior professional once again on the MCC 'A' tour to Pakistan. This proved to be his final tour in England colours, as by the mid-1950s Trevor Bailey of Essex became established as England's leading all-rounder.

Allan Watkins sweeps Surrey's McMahon for four at The Oval in June 1949.

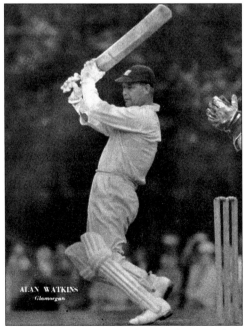

A rasping square cut from Allan Watkins against Essex in 1952.

However, Watkins continued to be a heavy scorer at county level, passing 1,000 runs in every season bar one from 1947 until 1960, as well as taking over 50 wickets in seven out of eight seasons between 1949 and 1956. Of his 29 centuries for Glamorgan, 28 were in Championship cricket, and in both 1947 and 1949, Watkins hit 4 centuries in the season.

Inevitably, these stoic efforts took their toll and by the early 1960s Watkins was increasingly troubled by asthma. He retired on medical advice midway through the 1962 season and took a warden's post at Usk Borstal. However, it was not long before he returned to cricket, acting as the coach at Christ College, Brecon and Framlingham, before moving to Oundle School, where he has been a very popular coach for many years. In 1991 Watkins became a life member of the MCC.

Ossie Wheatley

RHB and RFM, 1961-1970

Born: Low Fell, Durham, 28 May 1935

Batting career:

M	I	NO	Runs	Av
206	227	87	799	5.70
21	*11*	*4*	*20*	*3.33*

50	100	CT/ST
–	–	75
–	*–*	*6*

Bowling career:

O	M	R	W	Av
6262.2	1988	13356	715	18.67
201.0	*43*	*613*	*29*	*21.14*

5wI	10wM
37	4

Career best performances:
30 v Oxford University, Oxford, 1961
9/60 v Sussex, Ebbw Vale, 1968
4* v Lancashire, Southport, 1969
3/30 v Northants, Northampton, 1969

Ossie Wheatley led Glamorgan between 1961 and 1966 and his fast-medium bowling added an extra dimension to Glamorgan's attack throughout the 1960s.

He played a key role in Glamorgan's Championship win in 1969, as in the match against Essex at Swansea when his athletic fielding helped Glamorgan win a crucial game in a nerve-tingling situation. Essex's last pair were at the crease, needing three to win off the final ball, when Ray East played a deft late cut. The ball sped towards the third man boundary, but Wheatley ran along the ropes, picked up the ball and returned an arrow-like throw over the top of the stumps to run out John Lever. Not only did this give Glamorgan victory by one run, but it also put the county in a virtually unassailable position at the top of the Championship table.

Wheatley won Blues at Cambridge in 1957 and 1958, when he amassed a record 80 wickets for the university, thereby breaking a record which had stood since 1878. During that summer he showed a fine control of direction and length, with a highly effective away swinger, which often

moved late from the right-handers. After leaving university, he had a brief, but successful, career with Warwickshire, taking 110 wickets in 1960. In 1961 Wheatley was appointed as Wilf Wooller's successor to lead Glamorgan.

Over the next few years, he developed a most effective partnership with Jeff Jones, taking over 100 wickets in both of his first two seasons with Glamorgan and proudly led them to victory over the 1964 Australians. His best performances for Glamorgan ironically came in 1968, when he was initially drafted into the side after Jeff Jones was injured. Wheatley had only planned to play the occasional game in 1968, but after taking 9/60 against Sussex he stayed in the team to finished on top of the county's averages with 82 victims at 12 apiece and was one of *Wisden's* Cricketers of the Year.

He made a few more appearances in 1969, before retiring in 1970 to pursue business interests. He has remained involved with cricket, serving as a Test selector and being chairman of Glamorgan CCC, the TCCB's Cricket Committee and the Sports Council of Wales.

Tom Whittington

RHB and OB, 1901-1923

Born: Neath, 29 July 1881
Died: St Pancras, 19 July 1944

Batting career:

M	I	NO	Runs	Av
47	85	6	1152	14.58
(88	133	5	3363	26.27)

50	100	CT/ST
4	–	10
(13	4	31/1)

Bowling career:

O	M	R	W	Av
0.5	0	12	0	–
(13.3	3	54	3	18.00)

5wI	10wM
–	–

Career best performances:
60 v Hampshire, Southampton, 1922
(188 v Carmarthenshire, Llanelli, 1908)
(3/26 v Surrey 2nd XI, The Oval, 1904)

Tom Whittington's efforts off the field ensured that Glamorgan secured first-class status in 1921. The Neath-born batsman was a most influential figure in Glamorgan affairs either side of the Great War and, but for his efforts on and off the field, Glamorgan might never have entered the County Championship.

Born in 1881, he was the son of Dr T.P. Whittington, a Scottish rugby international who had played for the early Glamorganshire club. Tom subsequently read Law at Oxford and then secured a regular place in the Glamorgan side. In 1908 he took over the captaincy of the county XI and hit a career best 188 against Carmarthenshire at Llanelli. His efforts earned him selection for the Minor Counties and the MCC, with whom he toured the West Indies in 1910/11. He had a fine tour, scoring 685 runs, with 154* against British Guyana and 115* against All Jamaica, and he was selected again in 1912/13 when the MCC revisited the Caribbean.

Whittington took over the secretary's post with Glamorgan in 1909 and it was through the energetic efforts of the Neath solicitor that a campaign began to elevate the county into the first-class ranks. Whittington used his many contacts in South Wales to drum up financial support and, utilising his influence within the MCC hierarchy, he got their agreement to elevate Glamorgan to first-class status if they could secure home and away fixtures with eight other Championship teams. By the middle of 1920 he secured sufficient fixtures to allow Glamorgan's entry into the Championship.

Although he was almost forty, Whittington won a regular place in the Glamorgan side and acted as vice-captain in 1921. He took over the captaincy in 1922 and 1923, and proved to be a shrewd reader of the game. But playing resources meant that he never enjoyed as much success as he would have liked. Fortunately, Whittington had a good sense of humour and took the many rebuffs and critical comments with a wry smile.

Even Whittington became frustrated by the lack of success and, with his own batting form dropping off, he retired at the end of 1923 to take up a teaching post in Sussex. Whittington became Glamorgan's first-ever life member.

Born: Cardiff, 22 August 1953

Batting career:

M	I	NO	Runs	Av
65	73	22	502	9.84
64	*19*	*7*	*48*	*4.00*

50	100	CT/ST
2	–	19
–	–	*9*

Bowling career:

O	M	R	W	Av
1252.2	234	4204	135	31.14
446.0	*58*	*1804*	*84*	*21.48*

5wI	10wM
6	–

Career best performances:
70 v Nottinghamshire, Worksop, 1977
6/79 v Hampshire, Southampton, 1979
18* v Somerset, Sophia Gardens, 1978
5/17 v Worcestershire, Worcester, 1978

Alan Wilkins was a member of the 1977 Glamorgan side that played in the Gillette Cup final against Middlesex at Lord's. His lively left-arm seam bowling also played a key role in Glamorgan's progress to their first appearance in the final of a one-day competition at Lord's.

Wilkins had joined the county's full-time staff in 1977 after completing his studies at Loughborough University, and he soon proved to be a most effective and accurate change bowler, or new ball partner to the experienced Malcolm Nash. In the Gillette Cup quarter-final against Surrey at Sophia Gardens, the young bowler had an analysis of 12-3-33-2, dismissing Test players Graham Roope and Younis Ahmed during a controlled spell of accurate left-arm seam. He also excelled in the semi-final against Leicestershire at Swansea, with figures of 12-5-34-2, adding Brian Davison and Jack Birkenshaw to his list of victims.

Wilkins batted chiefly at number ten or eleven, but he could still play a capable innings, as shown in 1977 during the match with Nottinghamshire at Worksop, where he went in as nightwatchman in Glamorgan's second innings and proceeded to score a career best 70 before being trapped leg before by Bob White.

His most productive season in first-class cricket for Glamorgan proved to be 1977, with Wilkins taking 47 wickets, including five-wicket hauls at Portsmouth and Worcester. In 1979 he took 6/79 against Hampshire, but he only appeared in 10 first-class matches and at the end of the season moved across the Severn Estuary to join Gloucestershire. He made his debut for them in 1980 and took a career best 8/57 against Lancashire at Old Trafford in 1981.

Wilkins spent much of 1982 on the sidelines, before returning to Glamorgan in 1983. He added a further 12 first-class wickets to his tally and then retired from county cricket and emigrated to South Africa to start a new career in broadcasting. He returned to Wales in 1989 and has subsequently become a familiar face and voice on radio and television.

Lawrence Williams
LHB and RFM, 1969-1977

Born: Tonna, 20 November 1946

Batting career:

M	I	NO	Runs	Av
150	144	72	399	5.54
136	*55*	*30*	*102*	*4.08*

50	100	CT/ST
–	–	38
–	*–*	*14*

Bowling career:

O	M	R	W	Av
3535.4	816	9839	363	27.10
965.4	*109*	*3636*	*190*	*19.14*

5wI	10wM
13	1

Career best performances:
37* v Essex, Chelsmford, 1969
7/60 v Lancashire, Blackpool, 1970
10 v Kent, Swansea, 1973
5/30 v Hampshire, Bournemouth, 1972

Lawrence Williams, the fast-medium bowler from Tonna, still holds the record for the most number of wickets in a Sunday League season. In 1971 he took 33 wickets and returned several excellent spells, including 4/21 against Leicestershire at Neath and 5/31 against Surrey at Byfleet.

Williams had graduated from club cricket for Ynysygerwn and Gorseinon straight into Glamorgan's side in their Championship winning season of 1969. He made his first-class debut against Yorkshire at Swansea and finished the season with a highly creditable 56 wickets. Williams had few pretensions as a batsman, but in 1969 he scored a career best 37* against Essex at Chelmsford and shared a vital tenth-wicket partnership of 78 with Don Shepherd, which not only pulled the Glamorgan innings around, but gave them two valuable batting points in their chase for the county title.

His fast-medium seam bowling won him a regular place in the county's attack in the early 1970s, taking over 50 first-class wickets every season from 1969 until 1974. He proved to be a most effective foil to Malcolm Nash or Tony Cordle with the new ball, before reverting to a clever change bowler when the county signed Greg Armstrong, the West Indian quickie. His most productive season was in 1970, when he took 61 first-class wickets, although his best Championship performance came in 1973 when he returned match figures of 11/120 against Kent at Swansea.

Williams struggled with injury in 1975 and made just three appearances in first-class games. He also lost form in 1976, but even so, he was still quite surprised to receive a letter from the Glamorgan committee midway through the summer, warning him about his performance. Several players received similar letters and, like Williams, they too were shocked at this quite abrupt treatment. Williams decided to quit Glamorgan at the end of what had been a very troubled season for the county in 1976 and, had there not been so much angst off the field, Williams would surely have had a much longer professional career.

Wilf Wooller

RHB and RM, 1938-1962

Born: Rhos-on-Sea, 20 November 1912
Died: Cardiff, 10 March 1997

Batting career:

M	I	NO	Runs	Av
400	630	72	12692	21.60

50	100	CT/ST
61	5	392

Bowling career:

O	M	R	W	Av
9118.5	2332	23513	887	26.63

5wI	10wM
40	5

Career best performances:
128 v Warwickshire, Neath, 1955
8/45 v Warwickshire, Ebbw Vale, 1953

Whilst Maurice Turnbull was the architect of Glamorgan during the 1930s, Wilf Wooller was the man who laid the post-war foundations and watched the club flourish from 1948 when, under his astute leadership, the Welsh county won the Championship. Over the next fifty years, Wilf lived and breathed Glamorgan cricket, fulfilling almost every role within the club, from player to secretary and, latterly, as president.

Wooller learnt his cricket in North Wales, playing for Rydal School and Denbighshire, as well as having a brief trial with Lancashire Second XI. He was also a most talented rugby player, initially for Sale, and, after some impressive performances, the schoolboy was included in a Welsh trial in 1932/33. Remarkably, a fortnight later the sixth former won the first of his 18 caps by being a member of the first Welsh side to defeat England at Twickenham.

In the autumn of 1933, Wooller went to Cambridge, where he won Blues for both cricket and rugby, and continued to live life to the full. After leaving university, he worked in the coal trade, both in North Africa and in Cardiff, where he joined the city's famous rugby club. Initially, Wooller had little time for county cricket, playing just at the weekends for the St Fagan's club. Through a friendship with Maurice Turnbull, Wooller agreed to turn out for Glamorgan in 1938, when the side was badly affected by injury. He had an immediate impact, taking 5/90 on his debut against Yorkshire, and this refuelled his enthusiasm for the county game. The following year, the aggressive all-rounder hit 111 in two hours against the West Indies, which helped to set up a 73-run victory.

Wooller spent much of the Second World War in a Japanese POW camp and, when he returned to the UK in 1945, he tried to resume his sporting career. However, his loss of weight meant that he had to retire from club rugby, but he agreed to help Johnnie Clay rebuild the Glamorgan side. He took on various administrative and fund-

Wilf Wooller juggles with a catch against the Springboks at Swansea in 1951, watched by bowler Jim McConnon and fielders Allan Watkins, Phil Clift and Jim Pleass.

raising duties, before taking over the captaincy in 1947, moulding a successful squad with a mix of local talent and astute signings from other counties.

He was a ruthless – and at times very outspoken – captain, leading from the front and never afraid to ask anyone to do anything that he would not think twice about doing himself. Indeed, Wooller was ready to do anything in the side's best interest, whether it was opening the batting, bowling for hour after hour as a stock bowler, or fearlessly standing at short-leg, letting the opposition batsmen know what he thought of them! By sheer application and tenacity, Wooller made himself into an excellent all-rounder and a measure of both his ability and durability was that in 1954 he achieved the coveted double at the age of forty-one!

A measure of the high regard in which Wooller was held was that he acted as a Test selector from 1955 until 1962, during which time he also helped to choose a highly successful England side. In 1960 Wooller retired from playing for Glamorgan and took over as secretary. He mixed his administrative duties with sports journalism, becoming a respected writer on cricket and rugby for *The Sunday Telegraph*, as well as broadcasting for BBC Wales. His forthright views on air or in print showed that he passionately wanted to see Glamorgan become successful again. Despite several whiffs of controversy, his tenure as secretary saw Glamorgan defeat Australia on consecutive tours, win the County Championship in 1969, and reach the final of the Gillette Cup in 1977.